P9-BJQ-214

DISCARD

AFRICAN WOMEN IN THE
DEVELOPMENT PROCESS

AFRICAN WOMEN
IN THE
DEVELOPMENT PROCESS

Edited by

Nici Nelson

FRANK CASS

First published 1981 in Great Britain by
FRANK CASS AND COMPANY LIMITED
Gainsborough House, 11 Gainsborough Road,
London, E11 1RS, England

and in the United States of America by
FRANK CASS AND COMPANY LIMITED
c/o Biblio Distribution Centre
81 Adams Drive, P.O. Box 327, Totowa, N.J. 07511

British Library Cataloguing in Publication Data

African women in the development process.
  1. Women – Africa – Social conditions
  I. Nelson, Nici
  305.4'2'096   HQ1787

ISBN 0-7146-3175-2 (Case)
ISBN 0-7146-4032-8 (Paper)

This group of studies first appeared in a Special Issue on
'African Women in the Development Process' of *Journal of
Development Studies*, Vol. 17, No. 3, published by Frank
Cass & Co. Ltd.

Typeset by
Computacomp (UK) Ltd, Fort William, Scotland
Printed and Bound in Great Britain by
Robert Hartnoll Ltd., Bodmin, Cornwall.

Contents

Notes on the Contributors

Nici Nelson is an urban anthropologist who did her field work in Nairobi. She is a lecturer in the Anthropology Department at Goldsmiths' College, University of London. She has published a review of the literature on women in development in South Asia entitled *Why Has Development Neglected Rural Women?* as well as numerous articles on low income urban women in Africa.

Lourdes Benería was born in Catalonia, Spain, attended the University of Barcelona and Columbia University and is now teaching at Livingston College, Rutgers University. Her work has concentrated on the economics of education and labour and on women. She has published a book on women in Spain, *Mujer, Economia y Patriarcado durante el Periodo Franquista.* In 1977/78 she was coordinator of the ILO's Programme on Rural Women and has since then also been involved in research more directly related to women in the Third World.

Judy C. Bryson is a Freelance Consultant on Development Projects. B.A. International Relations, University of Denver, 1966; M.A. (Econ.) in Development Studies, Manchester University 1980. She served with the United States Agency for International Development in Washington D.C. and Ghana, 1966–1976, and is author of *Women and Economic Development in Cameroon.*

Elizabeth Gordon is a social welfare researcher in Jerusalem, Israel. Currently under contract to the Israel Ministry of Labour and Social Affairs, she is involved in teaching and research. From 1976 to 1978 she was a research fellow at the National University of Lesotho. Her paper, 'Easing the Plight of Migrant Workers' Families in Lesotho' is to appear in Böhning, Roger, ed, *Black Migration to South Africa: A Selection of Policy-Orientated Research,* Geneva: ILO, 1981.

Ilsa Schuster (Ph.D. University of Sussex, 1977) is Lecturer in Anthropology at the Universities of Haifa and Tel Aviv in Israel. She is the author of several articles on Zambian women and an ethnography, *The New Women of Lusaka* (Mayfield Publishing Company, Palo Alto). She lectured in African Studies at the University of Zambia.

Pat Caplan is Senior Lecturer in Anthropology at Goldsmiths' College, University of London. She has carried out field work in Tanzania (1965–7, 1976), in Nepal (1969) and in South India (1974–5). She has written *Priests and Cobblers: Social Change in a Hindu Village in West Nepal* (Chandler, 1972), and *Choice and Constraint in a Swahili Community* (IAI/OUP, 1975), and edited with Janet Bujra, *Women United, Women Divided, Cross-cultural perspectives on female solidarity* (Tavistock, 1978). She is currently working on a book on women's organisations in India.

Jennie Dey is currently a member of an Overseas Development Administration team assisting the Gambian government with drawing up a Food Strategy which is to be incorporated into the second Five Year Development Plan. She obtained her doctorate at Reading University in 1980 with a thesis, based on 20 months' field work in a Gambian Mandinka village, entitled 'Women and Rice in The Gambia: The impact of irrigated rice development projects on the farming system'.

Patricia Ladipo is a Research Fellow, Department of Extension Education and Rural Sociology, University of Ife, Nigeria.

Introduction

by Nici Nelson

Midway through the United Nations Decade for Women it seemed appropriate to coordinate a special issue for the *Journal of Development Studies* which concentrated on women's role in development processes. The World Conference in Mexico City in 1975 marked the beginning of a global examination of women's roles in the economic, political and social life of their societies and a recognition of their right to participate fully and equally in all aspects of society. Much has been written; many analyses presented. Some progress has been made in the area of formal development planning, for instance, the Basic Needs approach now in vogue for United Nations Agencies, and the Percy Amendment which makes it mandatory to include in each USAID feasibility study a consideration of the effects of that project on women in the 'target population'. However, as most of the articles in this volume confirm, a great deal more needs to be done. Women continue to be more underfed, undereducated, and overworked than men ... a neglected and under-utilized minority.

All of the articles in this Special Issue concentrate on sub-Saharan Africa, with the exception of Benería's paper 'Accounting for Women's Work' which is a general theoretical article. The decision was made to limit the discussion to Africa in order to provide a certain unity and cohesiveness to the issue. Attempting to examine such a broad subject for Africa alone is daunting enough; to try and do so for the world seems to defy reason. The cultural heterogenity would be too great.

Most of the articles (five out of eight) in this issue deal with specific situations in which African women find themselves, ranging widely from sub-elite nurses in Zambia to the efforts of uneducated women in Nigeria to form a cooperative. Two of these articles concern the effect of development projects on women. As an anthropologist I feel that analyses of objective conditions of development are important and necessary to delineate the circumstances under which women 'march forwards' rather than are 'pulled backwards' (see page 124). These articles attempt to do this for women in the African context.

Time and again the authors reiterate the point that failure to take cognisance of the crucial role women play in their societies and economies results in a serious loss of efficiency and productivity, to say nothing of simple human justice. One economist, two development consultants with anthropological training, one agricultural sociologist and four anthropologists consider various aspects of the development process and the ways women have contributed to or been affected by them. Three of the papers are general in nature, two being theoretical. Benería examines the nature and extent of women's participation in economic activities and the need to redefine economic activity to include production for use. Bryson considers current views on the division of labour in sub-Saharan African extensive and intensive agriculture and their implications for agricultural development. The third paper, by Nelson, is more practical in purpose, looking at the organisational and management difficulties which will be encountered by agencies which hire women project staff and involve village women in community participation exercises.

The remaining papers are profiles of women in different socio-economic contexts. Two papers analyse a particular socio-economic trend and its effect on women. Schuster critically examines the wholesale adoption of a western model of medicine and nursing in Zambia. Problems arise because nurses are imperfectly socialised into western-style ethics of medical care and feel an ambivalence toward their work. Gordon is interested in the situation in which the wives of migrants find themselves in Lesotho and whether they view their seemingly independent marital life positively or negatively.

Caplan's paper looks in detail at the implications for women's status and autonomy which a new government development policy on land and private housing could have in a coastal Tanzanian community. The last two papers take stock of two West African development projects. Dey has worked in a rice irrigation scheme in Gambia and Ladipo was part of the project staff of an experimental integrated rural development project run by the University of Ife in Nigeria, and looks at the differential results of the initial failure to integrate women into the development project.

As anthropologists or sociologists the contributors have presented critical analyses of the objective circumstances of women in particular times and places. Their interests are wider than the purely economic effect of development. They examine the social relations which change and are changed by development processes. They give due weight to the role which ideology can play in altering the direction of change (whether one is considering the ideology of the development experts or that of the local community). Finally, recognising the importance of understanding 'the view from the bottom' as well as that from the top, they have given where possible the perceptions of women themselves of development and the steps they are taking to achieve greater economic productivity and self-determination.

The contributions in this issue explore a number of common themes. The first is a consideration of the development process, how it is defined and then implemented. The second is the perceptions women have of development and the manner in which it impinges on their lives. The third is a consideration of ways in which development has benefited men more than women, increasing the inequalities of access to resources and opportunities existing between the genders. Fourthly, a minor theme, but one with serious implications for future research and analysis as well as development planning, is the critical examination of two concepts, work and the household. Lastly, all the contributors stress the need for development experts (whether planners, implementors or scholars) to give adequate and serious consideration to the crucial roles women play in their economies and societies.

What is Development?

In none of these papers is development defined explicitly, but each concerns itself with a different manifestation of this complex phenomenon. Schuster, Gordon and Bryson chose to look at development in its widest sense of growth and change brought about by a combination of political and economic forces operating on a country-wide or regional level. Change of this type is the result of local structures and conditions, colonial and neo-colonial experience, urbanisation and industrialisation as well as the policies of development planners. Caplan is explicitly concerned with the latter, a rural development policy and its possible effects on gender relations, family relations and marriages. Nelson is also interested in development policies from the viewpoint of the organisational implications of a commitment to involve women at all levels of development planning and implementation. Dey and Ladipo assess particular projects, one on-going project which made absolutely no attempt to involve village women and the other — a pilot project — where women themselves approached the project staff with a request to form cooperatives like their husbands. Implicit in the evaluations of various aspects of the development process is a model of development which emphasises equality of distribution of wealth and opportunity for all sectors of society in lieu of a strategy dedicated to increasing the Gross National Product (for such a definition of development see Seers [1974] and UNRISD [1977]). The significant difference is that here the authors concern themselves with equality of distribution of wealth and opportunity between the genders in the same class category (whether urban subelite or rural villager).

Most of the contributors had criticisms to make about the definition of development adopted by planners, politicians and academics. For example it is frequently the case that development is seen as a single, universal unvarying process (usually modelled after the Western experience, though members of other developed societies can be equally ethnocentric as Dey's article clearly demonstrates). This process frequently seems to be structured by men for men to which women must adjust without question. This assumption has a variety of repercussions. For example, in Zambia it meant the wholesale and unthinking adoption of western structures of medicine and a system of medical training which has not attempted to mediate between western and local views of sickness and medical care. The result has been imperfectly socialised Zambian women nurses who are asked to do what their concepts of ill health as well as their relatively powerless positions as young, unmarried women make virtually impossible.

Bryson also discusses a unitary view of development held by many economists and agricultural experts in which it is felt that intensification of agriculture in Africa means the automatic replacement of women in food crop production. She demonstrates that this has not been the case in the past and that there are strong social and ideological reasons (including factors of economic efficiency) why it will not occur automatically in the future.

Procedures for joining and participating in development projects are inflexible and standardized. The focus of development agents is to see how best women can adjust themselves to these procedures. Ladipo asks why it is not possible to plan in such a way as to modify the process appropriately. In the Nigerian experimental project one group of women adjusted to the rigid cooperative regulations while another modified the rules to fit their needs (for example, they formed a smaller than regulation group and lowered the requisite share payment). Needless to say the second group was more successful than the first. As Lapido says, too-rigid rules can limit imaginative growth. Nelson reiterates the same point, using as examples two Integrated Rural Development Programmes which developed flexible approaches in an effort to improve women's productive capacities.

Those who plan and implement development projects (and frequently those that do research on them) can thoughtlessly impose or assume the validity of their own concepts of social relations while introducing new technology. For example, the household is often defined as a unified productive unit under the control and direction of a single male head. Dey demonstrates the way in which the definition of the household, erroneously applied to rural Gambian society, had unfortunate repercussions on the successful implementation of a wet-rice project. Caplan feels that carrying out land registration and the 'house improvement' campaign in Tanzania assumes that families are now adhering to the more western model of small nuclear units each with a male head. She demonstrates how the traditional communal land ownership and flexible house types enable coastal Tanzanian women to retain a great deal of control over their sexual lives, marriages and living arrangements both in youth and old age. Changes in these institutions may well be a retrograde step which would deprive women of autonomy and self-determination.

On an analytical level, Benería shows that the household cannot be assumed to constitute an harmonious, homogeneous unit of consumption and production/ reproduction. The social relations between the individual members of the household must be examined carefully in each situation to determine the power hierarchies and lines of conflict in the household as well as the mechanisms and forms of subordination within it.

In addition Benería states that covering only measurable commoditised activity in the definition of economic activity is a reflection of western economic models where most economic work is translated into monetary terms. (Even in the West all 'work' is not so monetised and may be discounted by economists – witness the current debates on housework and reproductive labour.) To insist upon this circumscribed definition of 'work' in all societies results in a serious under-evaluation of women's economic contribution, giving an unrealistic picture of economic life which must skew planning, development programmes and employment policies.

Women's Perceptions of Development

Sandra Wallman has made clear that part of any process of change and development is the perceptions people have of it and the effect it has on their lives [1977]. Within a given society, there will be different perceptions and contradictory expectations which must be resolved [Wallman, 1977:49]. It is possible that women have different perceptions of development than men in the same society. Very little work has been done to clarify to what extent this is the case and what the implications of these different perceptions could be. If 'economic development as a variety of change creates a larger or different set of options or choices in a particular setting for particular categories of people' [ibid:61] then these societies must resolve the resultant conflict by defining meaning and value for the new alternatives. Conceivably, males and females, having differing access to the new options, could place different meaning and value to these alternatives. A situation of increasing tension and conflict between the genders would then result. The tense and conflict-ridden relations between the men and women have been commented on by observers and analysts of the African scene (too numerous to list here, but see Hafkin and Bay, Little, and Obbo). The articles presented here confirm this view and attribute the situation to women's unequal share of the new options or society's resentment when one group of women (as in the case of the Zambian nurses) has co-opted a large enough share to threaten the balance of power in gender relations.

All the contributors except for Benería consider to a greater or lesser degree women's own perceptions of development as it affects them. Some are more explicitly concerned with this problem. Gordon's paper is entirely focused on the perceptions of Lesotho migrants' wives and whether they find their relatively solitary responsibilities for family and farm a source of stress and anxiety or a means to freedom and independence. Schuster examines the ambivalent attitudes of Zambian nurses to their work and their reactions to the unfair demands made upon them by the public and medical institutions in the context of their training and work. Dey describes the problems besetting a Gambian wet rice scheme which arose in large part because the Chinese engineers who set up the project seriously misunderstood local division of labour patterns and household structures. She vividly portrays the rivalry between men and women over wet rice land, and the women's disappointment when they were passed over by the project organisers, even though wet rice cultivation was traditionally their responsibility. Ladipo presents a case study of groups of women in the University of Ife's pilot Integrated Rural Development scheme who objected because they felt that the new economic opportunities were being exclusively given to male heads of households.

The Effects of Development on Gender Relations

Most of these articles underscore with depressing predictability the ways in which the new economic opportunities have been controlled and co-opted by men. African men (as elsewhere) have moved into a more advantageous position vis-à-vis women in their respective communities over the past century. When cash crops were introduced they were grown and marketed by men, often to the detriment of their food crop production, as in Gambia when colonial officials intensified male groundnuts production for export (see Dey). In addition, men have often had the only opportunity to obtain wage employment. When they migrate to obtain this employment their rural families do not benefit greatly from the cash they earn (see Gordon for Lesotho). It is therefore no surprise that men have the best, if not the only, access to cash as the women in the Nigerian IRD scheme or the Niger IRAM programme discovered when they were asked to buy shares to join the cooperatives (see Ladipo and Nelson). Female de facto heads of households, as in Lesotho, may be expected to carry out their husbands' instructions on farm improvements and yet have no cash to do so (see Gordon). Men have also monopolised the new literacy and numeracy skills, as anyone attempting to organise a project run by women will soon discover (again, see Ladipo and Nelson). Men's activities have been modernised, streamlined, intensified and monetised; women's productive activities – usually the growing and processing of food crops, as well as the provision of the household's water and fuel – relatively less so, as Bryson makes abundantly clear. They may then be expected to provide labour on their husbands' cash crops, for their work load has been increased to an unacceptable level in many parts of Africa.

The realities of local life must be understood by development change agents, national and international, who have naïve hopes of 'improving the lot' of women. One of these is the nature of relationships of power between men and women. Women as daughters, wives and mothers may be under the social, if not the legal control, of fathers and husbands. Men may have the ability of preventing any activity which they suspect will undermine their authority over their women. Women's abilities, productivity and autonomy must be promoted in ways which do not threaten men overtly. For this reason Bryson feels that concentrating on those productive activities which were always women's concern is the most logical strategy to adopt in African development. Hence concentrating on the intensification of food crop production by women will improve the living standards of their families, give them access to cash (when they market their surplus production) and will not antagonise the men in the rural area.

It may be that in the initial instance, project organisers can only approach women with the permission of their men. This may mean holding a meeting to explain the project's objectives to the men of the village first and persuading them to allow the field staff to meet with their wives and daughters (see Nelson). In the Nigerian case men's agreements to cooperative activities had to be obtained and in one instance they refused to allow the women of a traditional triple village cluster to break their cooperative into the three constituent villages, since this would have threatened the traditional superiority of the largest village. In short, men's approval has to be sought as part of an on-going process of change: women's lives cannot be transformed in a vacuum and men must be brought along with the processes of transformation.

To do otherwise can have very unpleasant consequences. Women who defy the men in their society may obtain freedom and autonomy but can pay a high price. The Zambian nurses in Schuster's study suffered a great deal of public criticism not just because they could not deliver the proper type of medical care without breaking accepted mores of etiquette and modesty. These nurses have the income and the freedom to lead a free-wheeling life style; they enjoy spending their money on the 'good life' and having many men friends. For the first time sub-elite women are achieving a position by their personal efforts; of this achievement and their independence they are conscious and proud. Their life style and attitudes provide a model which threatens the system which is based on men's control of women's production and reproduction. As Schuster's other work on sub-elite Zambian women shows, such women's lives are not unmixed blessings and they can suffer a great deal in the climate of bitterness and distrust which marks relations between the genders and the generations.

Reconsideration of the Concepts of the 'Household' and 'Work'

Several of the contributors address themselves to the question of what is a household and how should it be defined by analysts and planners. Benería warns against assuming that the household is invariably a well integrated unit of distribution and production/reproduction in which relations between the adult members are well ordered and without stress. Looking at the household in cross cultural perspective it becomes quickly apparent that there is a wide variation in the manner in which production and distribution are organised within the household and forms that power relations between the genders take there. Caplan and Dey demonstrate the ways in which an imposition of the development experts' conception of the household can seriously affect women's productivity and autonomy. Gordon's article presents a very different look at the household in a situation where Lesotho women are forced by circumstances to be de facto heads of households without de jure rights or access to cash resources. Here (by an ironic twist) observers of this area of great male out-migration have assumed that the African extended family provides support and help to the wives left behind; an assumption which Gordon challenges. It is obvious that it is very important that the different types of household in an area be carefully examined, making sure that the outsiders' preconceptions are not imposed upon the reality. One cannot and should not assume that in any development process one need only deal with the household as a homogeneous unit under a single male head.

Similarly, misconceptions or preconceptions about what constitutes work can have serious repercussions on the way women's roles in their societies are assessed and the subsequent development policies built upon those assumptions. Just as we must give careful consideration to our definition of the household, so we must reconsider what is meant by work.

Women as a Neglected Resource

Increasing production and ensuring a more equitable relationship between the genders can only be achieved through consulting and involving women actively in development processes both at the planning and the implementation level. The contributions in this volume emphasise this point again and again. Failure to consult women about local family structures, land-holding patterns and division of labour led to inefficiency and lowered productivity on the Gambian rice irrigation scheme (Dey). Bryson feels that an inability on the part of those in authority to recognise the primacy of women in food crop cultivation has contributed to falling food production characteristic of many sub-Saharan African countries. The importance of female productivity to the nutrition and health of the household is stressed by several contributors. Development strategies which do not help women to improve their economic productivity neglect these important aspects of family life. Lastly development projects or processes which increase women's work load to an unacceptable level are not uncommon. All too frequently women find themselves working harder but having no greater control over their products or participation in family or community decision-making. Unless development planners and implementors consider equally the roles, views and values of both men and women, their policies, plans and projects will only serve to increase the inequalities which exist between the genders.

In Conclusion

It would be appropriate to close with a few words on Special Issues which deal with women. A glance at the Table of Contents of this Special Issue will show that all the contributors are women. This was not a conscious editorial decision. It merely reflects the sad fact that few men do research or analysis which gives equal weight to the consideration of the female half of the human race. Most development literature reflects this sexual segregation of research concerns. Claffey's review of 25 important works on Women in Development [1979] shows that there is only one male contributor (a co-editor). Other disciplines demonstrate the same inbalance, for example, a Special Issue on Women's Roles by the *International Journal of Intercultural Relations* had nine articles written from a wide variety of disciplinary approaches, all authored by women. Hafkin and Bay's *Women in Africa* had two male contributors (an unusually high proportion out of eleven).

What is most troubling about this segregation of interest is that it is a reflection of the fact that most academics and development experts (the majority of which are, after all, men) hold the view that anything concerned with women and development is a peripheral topic which can be safely left to caucuses of 'women's libbers' to discuss while they get on with the important issues. In the last ten to fifteen years excellent work has been done which has contributed to a more balanced consideration of both genders (in most academic disciplines as well as development studies). Yet it seems to have had very little impact on the orthodox mainstream of these disciplines (note Bryson's comment on the ignorance displayed by most agricultural and development economists on the realities of the agricultural division of labour in Africa).

There is a need to redress the balance of research concerns and to fill the information gap which exists about women in the development processes in the Third World. Special Issues provide a forum for accomplishing this objective. But when will the information gap be filled and will the time come when all researchers and development planners undertake their analyses and work in a way which gives full and equal consideration to people, all people?

REFERENCES

Claffey, J., 1979, 'Women in Development', *International Journal of Intercultural Relations*, Vol. 3, No. 4: 507.
Hafkin, N. and Bay, E., 1976, *Women in Africa*, Stanford, California: Stanford University Press.
International Journal of Intercultural Relations, 1979, Special Issue: Women's Roles: A Cross Cultural Perspective, Vol. 3, No. 4.
Little, K., 1973, *African Women in Towns*, Cambridge: Cambridge University Press.
Obbo, C., 1980, *African Women: Their Struggle for Economic Independence*, London: Zed Press.

Seers, D., 1974, 'Meaning of Development', *IDS, Communication Series*, No. 44.
UN Research Institute For Social Development, 1977, 'Monitoring Changes in the Conditions of Women: A Research Proposal'.
Wallman, S., 1977, *Perceptions of Development*, Cambridge: Cambridge University Press.

Conceptualizing the Labor Force: The Underestimation of Women's Economic Activities

This paper analyzes the concepts underlying existing labor force statistics and their built-in tendency to underestimate women's contribution to production. It argues that available statistics must be used with great caution and that differences in participation rates across countries can be misleading. The paper criticizes conventional definitions of economic activity and of labor force concepts; it suggests that use value production should be viewed as part of the economic realm and that labor engaged in it should be accounted for as 'active labour'. The main objective of this argument is to counteract the ideological undervaluation of women's work, and to present a concept of economic activity related to human welfare rather than to economic growth and accumulation.

I. INTRODUCTION

The growing amount of literature on women's issues that has appeared during the last ten years has been instrumental in deepening our understanding of the nature and extent of women's participation in economic activities. It has also increased our awareness of the conceptual and empirical problems that exist regarding this subject. One such problem is the definition and measurement of women's work. As studies on women's labor force participation have proliferated, the inadequacies of available statistics in capturing the degree of their participation in economic life has become progressively more obvious.

Survey work, detailed studies of women's activities, and even mere observation of everyday life has led to a general agreement about the obscurity and low value generally attached to women's work in most societies. There are in fact two issues that are inter-related along these lines. One is ideological and is associated with the tendency to regard women's work as secondary and subordinate to men's. An aspect of this tendency relates to the fact that an important proportion of women's work is unpaid. Both the ideological and monetary aspects are clearly symbolized by an expression such as 'my mother doesn't work' even though she might be working longer hours than any other household member. 'Work' in this case means participation in paid production, an income-earning activity. The

* The original research for this paper was carried out while the author was working as coordinator of The Programme on Rural Women of the International Labor Office. The views expressed here are the author's and do not necessarily reflect those of the ILO. A different version of this paper will be included in *Women and Development: The Sexual Division of Labor in Rural Societies* to be published by the ILO and edited by the author. Many thanks are due to the ILO colleagues who read the manuscript and helped at different stages of the project, in particular to Z. Ahmad, D. Ghai, F. Lisk, M. Loutfi and G. Standing, and to N. Nelson and G. Sen.

ideological aspect is reinforced by the pervasive lack of a clear conceptualization of the role played by women at different levels of economic life. For example, while an effort has been made to evaluate the contribution of subsistence agricultural production to, for example, national output, similar efforts to evaluate subsistence work carried out by women in the household have been the exception rather than the rule.

This ideological bias, as will be seen below, is deeply embedded in most of the concepts widely used in the social sciences; dealing with it requires an effort to analyze the very roots of this bias and to reconstruct these concepts in such a way that the role of women in society can be placed in its proper perspective. In the light of the arguments presented in this paper, it is ludicrous to include women among the 'passive' or 'inactive' groups in society such as pensioners, housewives and the handicapped [*Blanchard, 1979*]. (Note that Blanchard was speaking as Secretary General of the ILO, an institution highly concerned with refining labor force concepts and improving statistical information on the labor force.)

The second issue is a consequence of the first and is of a less fundamental but more practical nature. It refers to the actual statistical evaluation and accounting of women's work either as participants in the labor force or in terms of GNP estimations. It is by now well known that most labor force and national accounting statistics reflect a gross under-estimation of women's participation in economic activity. Concern over this problem has been growing during the past decade. Boserup, in her analysis of women's role in the development process, put it clearly when she wrote that 'the subsistence activities usually omitted in the statistics of production and incomes are largely women's work' [*1970:163*]. This concern has been expressed repeatedly by other authors as well: [*Gulati, 1975; Standing, 1978; UN, 1976*]. Yet subsistence production, as will be seen below, is not the only area of underestimation of women's work.

Although we do not want to fall into the trap of making a fetish of statistics, it is important to point out shortcomings of available data for the purposes of evaluating women's work. Those data are commonly used for planning purposes and can be the source of numerous biases. The purpose of this paper is to show how those shortcomings are rooted in the conceptual categories used. The focal point of the paper is the analysis of statistical biases and of the concepts that feed statistical categories. Part II analyzes the conventional definitions of active labor used, how they affect data collection and, more specifically, how they bias the evaluation of women as economic agents. Part III deals with the more theoretical aspects of the problem, linking these definitions to a given conceptual framework of what constitutes economic activity. A redefinition of economic activity is suggested and its implications for statistical purposes discussed in Part IV.

II. BIASES OF AVAILABLE STATISTICS

Until the Second World War, statistics on the 'economically active population' depended primarily on population censuses. The emphasis on problems of unemployment derived from the 1929 crisis and generated an increased interest in the collection of reliable statistics on the subject. In 1938 the Committee of Statistical Experts of the League of Nations recommended a definition of the concepts of 'gainfully occupied' and 'unemployed' population and drew up proposals to standardize census data with the purpose of facilitating international comparisons. As a consequence, many countries expanded the collection of statistics on what, from then on, would be called the 'labor force' [*ILO, 1976*; *League of Nations, 1938*].

The 1938 definition of gainful occupation was that 'for which the person engaged therein is remunerated, directly or indirectly, in cash or in kind'. The labor force was defined as comprising the gainfully occupied and the unemployed, the objective being to measure not only the employed population but the total labor supply. Updated labor force definitions adopted by the Statistical Commission of the United Nations in 1966 defined the economically active population as comprising 'all persons of either sex who furnish the supply of labor for the production of economic goods and services' [*ILO, 1976 : 32*]. The basic difference between the 1938 and 1966 definitions was that while the former responded to the objective of including the unemployed as forming part of the labor supply, the latter reflected an increasing concern not only with unemployment but also with under-employment. The objective was to reach an estimate of the potential labor supply in order to best estimate the under-utilization of labor resources; the potential labor supply was to include not only individuals contributing 'to the incomes of their families and to the national product' (p. 36), but also the unemployed and underemployed.

We can see from this definition that there are two focal points in the conventional measurements of the labor force. One reflects the concern over unemployment, the potential labor supply, and the full utilization of labor resources. The other reflects the link between the concepts of labor force and the national product – active labor being defined as that which contributes to the national product plus involuntary inactive or unemployed labor. Both lead to questionable measurements of the labor force – symbolized by the fact that a domestic activity such as cooking will be classified as performed by active labor when the cooked food is marketed and as inactive when it is not. And family members might be classified as underemployed when working in agriculture but not when engaged in household production.

This is because the underlying definition of the national product includes essentially only goods and services exchanged in the market. The problem of underestimation of the labor force is therefore more acute in areas where the market has not penetrated many spheres of human activity. While in industrialized societies the only major exception is domestic production – to the extent that it has not been commoditized[1] – non-market production is more prevalent in the Third World.

In order to deal with this problem, continuous efforts have been made, on the part of national and international bodies in charge of labor force statistics, to include non-market subsistence production in GNP estimations and subsistence workers as active labor.[2] Hence the introduction of the concepts of 'potential labor supply' and of 'marketable goods' in order to measure the contribution of some sectors not yet penetrated by the market. But despite the increasing sophistication in data collection and labor force estimations, important problems remain and the tendency to underestimate the active population – especially among women – is still a major flaw in available data. Let us examine more specifically the significance of these definitions from the point of view of measuring the female labor force.

The League of Nations 1938 definition specified that 'housework done by members of a family in their own homes is not included in that description of the gainfully occupied, but work done by members of a family in helping the head of a family in his occupation is so included, even though only indirectly remunerated' [ILO, 1976: 28–9] (emphasis added). Under this definition, when members of a household are assumed to help the head of the family (presumably a male), as for example agricultural workers, they are classified as 'unpaid family workers'; on the other hand, when the same individuals perform domestic work, such as food processing or water carrying, they are not defined as workers, the rationale being that the former are assumed to be engaged in income-earning activities while the latter are not.

Despite the considerable effort made since 1938 to improve labor force statistics, these concepts have remained essentially untouched to the present time; subsequent work has mainly concentrated on techniques of data collection. For example, the concern for estimating the potential labor supply reflected in the 1976 definitions had implications for female labor: 'Particular attention should be given to groups which may be especially difficult to classify, such as female unpaid family workers in agriculture ...' [ILO, 1976: 32]. However, the problem of underestimation of women's participation in the labor force has not disappeared, as a glance at the relevant ILO literature on the subject indicates [Standing, 1978, Standing and Sheehan, 1978]. Given the above definitions of the labor force, this underestimation is due to several factors.

First there is the problem of defining who is an unpaid family worker. In 1954, an ILO resolution recommended that, in order to be defined as such, an unpaid family worker must work in non-domestic activities for at least one third of the normal hours.[3] The problem of defining what are normal hours and for how long a family member has worked affects both male and female workers. A typical approach in many countries is that, in order to be classified as an active worker, an individual must have worked a minimum of 15 hours during the two weeks before a census takes place. However, given that involvement in home production does not merit inclusion in the 'labor force', and to the extent that women's unpaid family work is highly integrated with domestic activities, the line between what is conventionally classified as unpaid family worker and domestic worker becomes very thin and difficult to draw. The result is a logical underestimation of women's non-domestic work.

Second, when censuses classify workers according to their 'main occupation', the tendency to under-report women as workers in agriculture or any other type of non-domestic production is very prevalent. In India, for example, the 1971 Census excluded women whose main occupation was classified as housewife but who were also engaged in other work outside of the household; it has been estimated that, in this case, the exclusion of 'secondary' work implied a fall in the participation rate from almost 23 per cent to just over 13 per cent [Gulati, 1975]. The problem of under-reporting has been observed across regions, even though certain Moslem countries are often mentioned as extreme cases: 'With few exceptions, where censuses or surveys have been conducted in these countries ... the female unpaid family workers were, to a large extent, not recorded' [ILO,

1977, VI:11]. In Algeria, the number of women reported as unpaid family workers in the 1956 census was 96,000; after a post-census re-evaluation of data, it was estimated that 1,200,000 women working as unpaid family members had not been reported [*ibid*].

There are several reasons for this under-reporting: they range from the relative irregularity of women's work outside the household – that is, the greater incidence among women of seasonal and marginal work – to the deeply ingrained view that women's place is in the household. If census and survey workers do not ask about primary and secondary occupations, they are likely to classify a good proportion of women as working only in the household when this is not actually the case. In many countries it is considered prestigious to keep women from participating in non-household production;[4] when asked whether women do so both men and women tend to reply negatively even if this is not the case. In addition, under-reporting might be due to any economic incentive derived from 'hiding' women's income earning activities – such as the loss of paid security benefits and family subsidies tied to the full time dedication of the housewife to domestic activities [*Benería, 1977*].

Thirdly, some activities are performed by women at home even though they are clearly tied to the market. This is the case when they sell food and drinks in or near their own home. Cloth-making for non-family members and selling of handicrafts and other products inside the family compound are other examples. The proximity and integration of these activities with domestic work makes them highly invisible too; they are likely to go unreported as market activities unless census and survey researchers are conscious of the problem.

Consequently, conventional labor force statistics must be approached with a high degree of skepticism when evaluating women's participation in production. Women working as wage laborers will tend to be automatically classified in the labor force, but women working in agriculture or in any other activity not clearly connected with the market might not be – depending upon each country's definition of labor force and upon methods followed to estimate it.

Table 1 provides an illustration of available figures on regional and country activity rates. Compiled by the ILO, they are drawn from country surveys and censuses, and widely used for international comparisons of labor statistics. Table 1 shows that activity or labor force participation rates (the proportion of the population classified as gainfully occupied and as unemployed) are much higher for men than for women across regions. It also shows that variations in activity rates are higher among women; while the lowest average regional rate corresponds to Latin America, the highest rates, for the three years given, are registered for the more industrialized countries of Europe and North America. Given the very high degree of involvement of women in agricultural production and trade in many African countries, the relatively low rates shown for Africa might immediately be questioned. However, the degree of variation is greater among countries, especially when differences between age groups are taken into consideration. For example, activity rates for the 25–44 age group in 1970 ranged from 4.2 per cent in Saudi Arabia to 67 per cent in Zaire and 93 per cent in the USSR [*Benería, forthcoming*]; and [*Standing, 1978*].

These figures should only be read as rough estimates of women's labor force participation rates. For example, the very low activity rates reported for the Arab

TABLE 1

ACTUAL AND PROJECTED ACTIVITY RATES, BY REGION (PER CENT)

	Males			Females		
	1975	1985	2000	1975	1985	2000
Asia	53.8	53.1	54.0	29.1	28.4	28.2
Africa	51.6	49.3	47.8	24.4	22.9	22.0
Europe	58.2	58.5	56.9	31.4	33.0	34.3
Latin America	48.9	48.0	48.5	14.0	15.4	18.3
Northern America	56.3	57.4	57.4	32.2	34.3	37.2
World	53.8	53.0	53.0	29.1	28.2	28.2

Source: ILO, *Labour Force Projections, 1977.*

countries should not be taken at face value. A census taken in Sudan in 1956, which included questions about both primary and secondary occupations, resulted in a labor force participation rate of women of almost 40 per cent [*Standing, 1978:29*], in contrast with other official statistics that report rates barely above the 10 per cent level.

In a survey taken by Deere in the Andean region, it was found that the proportion of women participating in agricultural work was 21 per cent instead of the 3 per cent officially reported [*Deere, 1977*]. This type of underestimation is common across countries, and especially in agricultural areas [*Anker and Knowles, 1978*; *ILO, 1978*]. To the extent that the amount of agricultural work that women perform is greater for the poorer strata of the peasantry [*Deere, 1978*; *Stoler, 1976*; *Young, 1978*], it implies that this underestimation differs according to class background and affects women from the poorer strata to a greater degree.

Two conclusions can be drawn from this. One is that studies on women based on conventional labor force statistics must use a great degree of caution in their analyses and inferences about women's work. The danger of tautological conclusions is obvious: if active labor is primarily defined in relation to the market and if production and labor not clearly exchanged in the market tends to be grossly underestimated, the positive relationship often found between women's activity rates and some index of economic development is clearly erroneous. This is especially the case when comparing predominantly agricultural with predominantly industrial countries and geographical areas. Yet numerous studies on women's labor force participation continue to ignore the problem.[5]

In addition, the implication often derived from this positive relationship, namely that economic development and industrialization have positive effects on women's emancipation, is far from being obvious. This is not just because women's participation in production and control over resources in less economically developed agricultural societies might be greater than statistics lead us to believe [*Boserup, 1970*; *Bukh, 1979*; and *Rubbo, 1975*]. It is also because, although participation in the industrial/urban labor force might provide women with a source of earnings, participation per se does not guarantee freedom either from subordination to patriarchal structures or from other forms of exploitation [*IDS Bulletin, Vol. 10, No. 3, 1979*].

The second conclusion is that the great disparity in women's participation in the labor force across countries is likely to be exaggerated and international comparisons likely to be misleading as long as a comparable statistical base is not adopted. Although country and regional differences do exist, comparisons based on figures such as official female labor force participation rates must be qualified with a scrutiny of data collection in each country. In addition, it is necessary that the concepts that have nourished statistical definitions be clarified. It is to this subject that I turn now.

III. THE CONCEPT OF ACTIVE LABOR

The problem of underestimation of women's work becomes even more acute if we question the conventional definitions of active labor. It is at this level that the ideological dimension in the evaluation of women's work comes in. The basic question arises from the need to define who is engaged in the production of goods and services during a given time-reference period. (See the definition by the Statistical Commission of the U.N. given above.) In the last resort, it amounts to defining what constitutes an 'economic activity' and understanding the conceptual and functional boundaries between it and other types of activity.

For orthodox economics, the focal point for the analysis of economic activity is the process of capitalist growth and accumulation, with emphasis given to quantitative relations in commodity production. The basic mechanism through which these relations are expressed is the market which becomes the formal expression of economic activity. Through the process of exchange, the price of commodities is an indicator of their relative worth. Market exchange is tied to the division of labor which, as A. Smith typically emphasized, is viewed as the basis for productivity increases and as the source of the wealth of nations. The production of exchange values is viewed as economic activity whereas use value production is normally not viewed as such. Exchange values take their concrete form through the market and, in that sense, the market becomes the basic source of information for a quantitative evaluation of society's output.

This explains why orthodox economics focuses its attention on the market; although the economic system is regarded, as Robbins has put it, 'as a series of independent but conceptually discrete relationships between men (sic) and economic goods' [1932:69] these relationships are viewed essentially from a quantitative perspective. In fact the almost exclusive attention paid to quantitative relations in neo-classical economics has often led to identifying these relations with the essence of economic analysis.

It follows from this that activities falling outside the market mainstream are considered peripheral to the economic system and not defined as 'economic'. The history of national income accounting and of labor force statistics, as explained in the previous section, has followed this basic theoretical framework. Efforts to incorporate 'marketable goods' in national income accounts represent an attempt to apply this framework to non-market activities. In the same way, when home-based activities produce goods for exchange, they become 'income-earning activities' and the labor engaged in them, active labor. That is, *when work becomes commoditized*, in the sense that it produces goods and services for exchange, *it is regarded as an economic activity; participation in the labor force is then measured in terms of labor's links with market activity*.

Within the non-orthodox tradition, these concepts have often been used in a similar way despite basic differences with the orthodox tradition. Marxists, for example, have argued that economics cannot be confined to the sphere of quantitative relations between people and economic goods, and that social relations underlying commodity exchange need to be considered as part of the economic realm; as Sweezy has pointed out, 'the quantitative relation between things, which we call exchange value, is in reality only an outward form of the *social* relation between the commodity owners' (p. 27). However, despite the fact that Marx talked about all labor producing use-values as productive labor,[6] the most prevalent position within the Marxist tradition has been in accordance with his contention that 'use value as such lies outside the sphere of political economy' [*Marx, 1911:19*]. Sweezy explains this exclusion of use value production from the field of investigation of political economy on the grounds that Marx 'enforces a strict requirement that the categories of economics must be social categories, i.e., categories which represent relations between people' (p. 26).

The reason for this exclusion must be sought in Marx's concentration on the analysis of the capitalist mode of production and the dynamics of accumulation. Thus, despite the broader definition of economic categories within the Marxist framework, a relative neglect of non-commoditized sectors – such as subsistence production and the household economy – has been a common feature until recently.

During the past few years there has been an increasing realization of the importance of understanding the nature and significance of non-commodity production and its role within the economic system. What is argued in this section can be summarized in two points: (1) use value production *does* embody a social relation and should therefore not be excluded from the field of political economy; (2) exclusion of use-value production renders the analysis of economic activity incomplete, leads to distortions in the measurement of the labor force, and can reinforce ideological biases related to the undervaluation of women's work. The central argument of this paper is that any conceptualization of economic activity should include the production of both use and exchange values, and that active labor should be defined in relation to its contribution to the production of goods and services for the satisfaction of human needs. Whether this production is channeled through the market and whether it contributes directly to the accumulation process are questions that can be taken up at a different level of analysis and should not affect our understanding of what constitutes economic activity. The argument is far from implying that there is no difference between commodity and non-commodity production, but rather that the latter type of production is also part of the realm of economics and must be valued accordingly.

The basis for this argument is provided by the literature on domestic work, reproduction and subsistence production which has been developed during recent years. In what follows, I present a brief summary of the contributions that are relevant for the purpose of this argument.

(i) Domestic Work and Subsistence Production: The End of Invisibility

The analysis of the household has gradually increased in sophistication over recent years. Within the field of economics,[7] neoclassical analysis pioneered this effort with theoretical and empirical work on the factors effecting women's participation in paid production. Further work along these lines was concentrated on subjects such as the quantification of domestic production through time-allocation studies, the estimation of the market value of home production, fertility analysis, and the economic factors affecting marriage and divorce. This work has centered around the application of utility maximization and cost-benefit analysis to the domestic economy. That is, it has applied conventional micro-economics to the analysis of the household, with an emphasis on quantitative relations.

In contrast, feminist and Marxist literature has centered on the significance of unpaid household production for an understanding of the economic role of women both within the household and the larger economy, and of its implications for an understanding of the reasons behind women's subordination. It has emphasized the role of women in the reproduction and daily maintenance of the labor force – a fundamental point made being that household production cheapens the costs of maintenance and reproduction. This is so in comparison with the costs that would be incurred if the goods and services produced domestically with unpaid labor were bought in the market. Household production therefore reduces labor costs in commodity production and, in this sense, can be regarded as having, if not a *direct* link with it, an *indirect* effect on the accumulation process [*Beechey, 1977; Deere, 1976; Fee, 1976*].

Two basic differences between the two approaches can be pointed out. One is that while orthodox economics, in applying the concepts used in market-oriented micro-economics to the domestic economy, tends to blur the distinction between use values and exchange values, feminist and Marxist analyses have stressed this distinction. The other concerns the political significance of the analysis; while conventional analysis takes the economic system *uncritically* and tends to *describe* changes taking place within it, the second approach asks political questions more directly and emphasizes the link between women's roles and the economic system. These questions are formulated both from the point of view of examining women's subordination to men – a problem that can apply to any given economic and political system – and from the point of view of seeking to understand how this subordination is integrated with exploitation in class society.

Yet both approaches share a common result: domestic labor and its connections with the non-domestic economy are no longer invisible. The incorporation of domestic work in the mainstream of analysis reflects the progressive realization of its importance for a full understanding of women's work and of the sexual division of labor in and outside of the household.

Similarly, the analysis of the subsistence sector and of the role that it plays within the larger economy has recently received new attention. This analysis has raised further important questions. Many authors have pointed out the permanence of this sector in many countries of the Third World, not only in agricultural areas, but also in urban areas under the form of a marginalized population which is either not absorbed by the capitalist sector or repelled by it as unemployed labor. Yet subsistence production is *indirectly* related to market production. As Wolpe has argued in relation to South Africa, the existence of the subsistence sector allows the capitalist sector to pay a wage which covers only the subsistence needs of the wage laborer – normally a male migrant – instead of family subsistence. The role of women in providing unpaid work within this sector, in domestic and agricultural production, and in cheapening the wage has also been pointed out by other authors [*Bukh, 1979; Deere, 1976; Mueller, 1976*]. The subsistence sector constitutes therefore a source of cheap labor from which wage labor can be drawn as capital accumulation proceeds. Far from being two separate sectors, as the dual economy analysis argues, the subsistence and the capitalist sectors are highly interconnected to the extent that the latter feeds upon the former.

Use-value production outside of market exchange takes place both in the household and in the subsistence sector. Efforts have been made to include it in GNP calculations[8] even though its market value is difficult to estimate. In particular, agricultural production not exchanged in the market is viewed as 'marketable output' and labor engaged in it as being part of the labor force – as the concept of 'family worker' indicates. Problems of underestimation in this case are due to practical difficulties in data collection, not to conceptual biases.

In contrast, the few attempts made at estimating domestic production have for the most part not generated a clear definition of household production as an economic activity and especially of domestic workers as being part of the labor force unless they be wage workers. In the last resort, housework is linked with consumption rather than with production by most authors. Galbraith, who included a chapter on 'Consumption and the Concept of the Household' in his *Economics and the Public Purpose*, regards housework as 'the labor of women to facilitate consumption' [*1973:33*]. Yet, part of the recent literature on domestic labor contains a clear conceptualization of domestic work as an integral part of the economic system. Within the Marxist tradition, several authors have discussed the need to view the concept of mode of production as including 'the relations and forces involved in the production of use values but also those involved in the reproduction of the species [reproduction of people]' [*Himmelweit and Mohun, 1977*]. However, in the last resort housework is linked with consumption rather than with production since it concerns 'production of use values for immediate consumption outside of any direct relation to capital' (p. 28). While this point is important for the purpose of differentiating use value from exchange value production and of delineating what activities contribute directly to the process of capital accumulation, it does not justify the asymmetry in the conceptual treatment given to the two types of use value production. Although it is important to differentiate between activities directly related to capital and activities that are not, and between labor that participates in the commodity sector or not, this does not justify the exclusion of any type of non-commodity production from our definitions of economic activity and active labor.

In the conventional definitions of national product and labor force, the rationale for this asymmetry seems to be the assumption that subsistence agricultural production consists of goods normally sold in the market while household production does not. Yet this assumption becomes even more arbitrary when household production is looked at from an historical perspective. The extent and nature of household-related work – overwhelmingly women's work across countries – varies according to the stage of economic transformation of a given society. The gradual penetration of the market into economic life generates a shift of production from the domestic to the market sphere of production. In industrialized societies, where subsistence depends predominantly on the wage, the function of domestic work is to 'transform' family income into consumable goods and services, only a small part of which is produced within the household. The burden of subsistence therefore falls on the wage, parts of production get gradually removed from the household, and domestic labor tends to concentrate on the transformation of market goods for household consumption.

By contrast, domestic labor in predominantly agricultural societies contains a higher degree of production − as symbolized by the fact that all stages of food transformation are often carried out in the household. In addition to strictly domestic activities, women's work around the household consists of a great variety of subsistence activities − such as water carrying, wood gathering, and food transportation − which often require long hours of work. The burden of subsistence in this case falls on these types of activities together with agricultural work in which women's participation is also high. In this case, agricultural and household-related tasks are highly integrated in time and space, and productive and reproductive activities highly intertwined. The introduction of the notion of 'marketable goods' in such cases for the purpose of evaluating subsistence production and measuring the labor force constitutes a projection of a concept specific to commodity production for the purpose of differentiating two types of output − marketable and non-marketable. These in fact serve similar functions and can hardly be separated out. The gradual penetration of the market into rural economies introduces different degrees of direct contact with commodity production and capital. Yet it does not change the productive and reproductive *nature* of these activities; what changes is the degree of their integration into commodity production and into the economic system.

(ii) Social Relations and Use Value Production

Now that domestic and subsistence production are becoming analytically more visible, and their proper role within the economic system is being re-evaluated, it is increasingly difficult to argue that the production of use values does not embody a social relation. The penetration of analysis into the household and subsistence production has been instrumental in bringing into the open the complexity of 'social relations' in use value production. We can talk, for example, about differences in access and control over the household means of production and about the unequal distribution of resources among different household members − as some empirical studies have documented [*Longhurst, forthcoming*]. A closer analysis of differences in household organization also documents the complexity of relations in regard to household hierarchies by sex and age and of the division of labor even among members of the same sex [*Benería, 1979*]. Similarly, under a wage labor system in which subsistence depends on the male wage, we can identify, as Seccombe has done, two levels of exchange − between employer and wage laborer and between wage laborer and domestic worker − existing in the interaction between the household economy and commodity production. Thus, it is logical to view the two levels of exchange as generating a set of social relations. In the same way, social relations are generated in the interaction between domestic and agricultural production in a subsistence setting to the extent that these activities can be viewed as part of the agricultural production process, when women cook and carry meals to the men working in the fields.

Two different conclusions spring from these observations. One is that the assumption of the household as the most basic unit of analysis – which is often made in the social sciences – is not appropriate. The household cannot, for example, be assumed to be a harmonious unit of consumption and production/ reproduction; it is precisely the conflicting nature of the relations generated by these functions that is being disentangled by feminist analysis. And this implies that it is important to distinguish between the household as a collective unit and the individual members that are part of it. This is especially so if our interest focuses on the analysis of mechanisms and forms of subordination/domination.

The other implication is that the household cannot be viewed as being isolated in the 'private' sphere and distinct from the 'public' sphere. Both spheres are highly interconnected and have an influence upon each other. Once the role of use value production and its importance within the larger economy is understood, the separation between the two spheres becomes artificial. It is in fact this separation which is at the root of the asymmetric treatment given to different types of use value production.

A full understanding of these implications leads to the conclusion that whether we are dealing with agricultural production or domestic work within either a polygamous household or the nuclear family, use value production generates 'social relations between people' and forms part of 'the categories of economics'. Once this is understood it is still possible to differentiate between activities that are *directly* related to capital accumulation and those that are not, or between that part of the labor force that produces exchange values and the part that is engaged in use value production.

IV. MEASURING WOMEN'S WORK

The purpose of the previous section was to discuss the concepts that underlie economic categories and to present a framework that can move us beyond conventional concepts of the labor force. Practical implications for data collection and statistical evaluation of women's work can follow from new concepts. But first we might ask about the usefulness and significance of such an exercise. The two main questions here are *why* do we want to expand our concept of active labor to include use value production and, especially, *what difference* can it make for women. Obviously it is possible that censuses and survey work might be addressed to evaluate all economic activities, as defined above, and yet be totally irrelevant for dealing with women's subordination.

Having recognized this possibility, I want to argue that such an exercise responds to three main objectives. One is to counter-act the ideological undervaluation of women's work and to give recognition to the long hours of labor in which women are engaged. We are in fact only arguing that domestic labor should receive the same treatment as other types of labor engaged in use value production. But, in addition, we are also underlining the crucial function played by women within the larger economy and pointing out the interaction between use value and commodity production.

The argument presented here should not be taken as a tacit acceptance of the traditional sexual division of labor by which women remain predominantly in unpaid work. What is intended is to focus on the economic significance of this work and to point out, for example, that women clearly engage in a 'double day' load when they are responsible for household duties in addition to a similar load to men's outside of domestic production. This implies that it is essential to understand that it is not enough to emphasize the need to increase women's participation in paid production as a basis for their economic self-reliance; any development scheme, be it a limited employment policy or an ambitious radical change, must deal with the question of how to organize production so that women are not burdened with a double load.

A second objective is related to the simple need to have as much information as possible about women's activities and their role in economic life. Planning, development programs, employment policies, training and educational programs, introduction of technological change at all levels (including the household), etc., must be based on accurate information on women's work if they are to be fully relevant to about 50 per cent of the world's population.

A typical example of the need for more information is the problem of unemployment and underemployment among women. The lack of accurate estimations of these variables in most countries is a natural consequence of the problems described so far; if women are either not classified or underestimated as workers, it is logical that they will also be underestimated among the unemployed since, in order to be counted as such, they must first be defined as part of active labor. Some hints at the high underemployment and unemployment of women in the Third World exist,[9] but for the most part systematic information on the subject is not available. In the industrialized countries, unemployment rates among women are higher than among men practically across the board. Yet this type of information should be a starting point of any development strategy and employment policy. This information cannot be obtained accurately without an estimation of the proportion of women that are 'taking refuge' in domestic and subsistence production because there is no employment elsewhere available to them.

Finally, a third objective in expanding our concept of active labor is to define economic activity in such a way as to relate it to human welfare rather than to a given process of growth and accumulation. As pointed out earlier, it is important to focus on commodity production if we are interested, for example, to understand the process of production and growth in a capitalist economy; a different question is to move beyond commodity production and focus on all activities contributing to the satisfaction of material needs − as required, for instance, by a basic needs development strategy. By differentiating between the broader level of economic activity and the narrower level specific to a given process of growth and accumulation, we are differentiating between all activities contributing to human welfare and those linked to a particular economic system. In this way, we transcend the conceptual framework that evolved out of the specific categories linked to capitalist production, of labor put to use for accumulation and profit.

We must now examine the pragmatic implications of the arguments made in this paper for statistical work lest we be charged with being impractical. It should be pointed out that some of the discussion carried out by the ILO on the issue of labor force statistics and by neoclassical economists working on household time-use data comes close to asking some of the questions posed in this paper. The issues raised include the difficulty of drawing a dividing line between economic and non-economic activity, and the distinction between economic activity and housework.[10] Some authors have talked about *economic activities* that are 'marginal' (such as hunting, handicrafts and raising vegetables) and 'auxiliary' (repairing tools for one's work and marketing home-produced goods) which are not likely to be included in labor force statistics unless they are clearly performed for the market [*Mueller, 1978*].

In one ILO recommendation on household survey statistics of the labor force, it is suggested that data collection should concentrate on 'how people earn their living' [*Turvey, 1978*]. The difficulty, however, appears where we want to be more specific about what earning a living means. While some authors have insisted on concentrating on income-earning activities, i.e., on following a market-oriented bias, others suggest that the number of hours of work can be used for an indication of work for a living – which implies that work might not produce an income but is implicitly a part of 'economic activity'. The exact meaning of economic activity is never defined, but what is made clear is that there are problems with the conventional definitions and that an understanding exists of the fact that many tasks performed in and around the household are related to 'earning a living'.

If we use the expression 'make' instead of 'earn' a living, it is even clearer that very little difference exists between the various types of subsistence and domestic activities with regard to their contribution to making a living. A similar argument can be made for activities such as food processing, cooking, washing, repairing the house, and taking care of the aged. If in addition we add reproductive tasks as an integral part of the overall process of production/reproduction, we are adding activities such as the care of children to the above list. Taken together, they include all use value production – of tangible goods as well as services. On the other hand, the list would not include non-work activities such as recreation and leisure.

For statistical purposes, an evaluation of use value production and of the labor force participating in it requires a detailed investigation of the tasks and the work involved. Survey research carried out at the household level and the subsistence sector has pioneered the type of research that is necessary. However, what is also needed is a systematic data collection by country that can provide a continuous source of information and that is moderately standardized. One of the problems that immediately comes to mind is how to measure work and labor participation. Use of number of hours of work might be misleading since, given the flexibility of scheduling in subsistence and domestic tasks, work can be carried out with different degrees of intensity, interspersing it with leisure time, with breaks of different duration, etc. This makes it difficult to measure not only labor force participation but also underemployment and labor utilization.

One possible way to deal with these questions is the estimation of the *average* number of hours that household members spend in use value production – the average based on survey work and depending upon the specific characteristics, such as the level of technology, and the extent of use value production in each country. For those who might be skeptical about estimating an average, it should be pointed out that evidence exists to show that the amount of time spent on domestic work has not changed considerably through time and has been found to be very similar in countries with very different socio-economic characteristics;[11] the variations among countries and through time are related to the *composition* of housework and the *duration* of specific tasks. Thus, while shopping is more time-consuming in some countries, less time is spent on other activities such as taking care of children or cleaning. Averages can take into consideration other differences such as those between rural and urban households and variations by class.

However, the use of averages should be accompanied by detailed information about the composition and duration of specific tasks. In particular, classification of work and activities can respond to a range of questions:

(a) Overall, we want to know the involvement of household members in use value production. In particular, the objective is to evaluate women's participation in all tasks contributing to production and reproduction.

(b) The distinction between commodity and use value production can be made clear by distinguishing between income-generating tasks and production for the household's own consumption. To the extent that conventional estimations have included subsistence agricultural production in labor force and GNP calculations, they do not totally coincide with the category of commodity production which is directly tied to the market and to capital. These estimations often blur rather than clarify the distinction between commodity and use value production. The distinction can be made clearer if statistical data are gathered with this purpose in mind.

(c) This distinction is also important for the purpose of measuring unemployment; questions can be drawn up in such a way as to determine whether a worker, male or female, is 'taking refuge' in the subsistence or domestic sector due to a lack of employment opportunities in the commodity sector, and this requires a clear distinction between these sectors.

(d) Further breakdown of activities in different categories can provide information for a variety of purposes. Thus, tasks related to reproduction will provide information about demographic factors, child care and schooling needs, time spent in shopping and food transformation, the effect of household technology on domestic work, the need for community services, etc.

This list is not meant to be exhaustive but to illustrate at the general level the type of data collection that can be taken for a full account of women's work (as well as of other household members, such as children and the aged, whose activities are also underestimated). This account per se tells little about the mechanisms of subordination that this work might entail, but it can provide basic information to pursue the analysis of women's position in society.

V. CONCLUDING COMMENTS

I have argued in this paper that, within conventional definitions of labor force, women's participation in economic activities tends to be grossly underestimated, particularly in areas with a relatively low degree of market penetration in economic life. This is due mostly to conceptual and ideological biases concerning the nature of women's work and to difficulties in collecting accurate statistics of their labor force participation. As a result, available information on women's work must be used with caution and international comparisons in particular can be very misleading if the statistical concepts and data collection methods used by different countries are not taken into account.

The main thrust of the paper, however, is to point out the shortcomings of conventional labor force concepts. These concepts are geared to measuring labor participation in commodity production, that is, in production for exchange instead, for example, for the satisfaction of basic human needs. The reason for this bias is to be found in the view that economic analysis and economic categories have been defined in relation to the process of growth and accumulation; only workers engaged in activities *directly* related to that process are conventionally defined as being in the labor force. The main argument of this paper is that active labor should include all workers engaged in use value as well as exchange value production which includes activities such as household production and all types of subsistence production. At a more concrete level, narrower categories of labor can be distinguished – such as labor engaged in commodity production and that which is not. Within a capitalist economy, this implies that the concept of active labor goes beyond labor engaged *directly* in capitalist production for the market.

From the point of view of women's work, the purpose of this conceptualization was underlined in the previous section and can be summarized under two main objectives. One is *ideological* and it has to do with the proper evaluation of women's work and the eradication of sexist concepts. A full understanding of the economic significance of household production, for example, implies that women's work is economically productive and essential for the functioning of the economic system. Society as well as women themselves must recognize this function in order to avoid succumbing to the view that it is of secondary importance, a basic source of women's subordination. This can remove the paradox, so commonly found in the Third World, in which a local economy survives thanks to women's involvement in subsistence production while men are unemployed; yet official statistics show low labor force participation for women and high participation for men respectively.[12] The other objective is of a *practical* nature and concerns the dynamics of change: a more general definition of labor force implies that development strategies and programs of action must be concerned with the whole spectrum of active workers. Thus the introduction of more productive technology in household production will free household workers from time-consuming tasks while widening the range of possibilities of choice between domestic and non-domestic work. Similarly, employment programs must take into consideration the degree of unemployment and underemployment 'hidden' in use value production. Under conventional statistics unemployed women who concentrate on household activities due to lack of opportunities to work outside the household are not included in the category of 'discouraged workers', nor as 'unemployed'. The implications of this paper indicate that they are part of the labor force and should be a matter of concern for any employment program.

NOTES

1. Throughout this paper, the concept of commodity is used in its usual meaning of an output produced for the purpose of being exchanged in the market and sold for a price.
2. The ILO, for example, has maintained a continuous interest in devising new approaches to deal with the problem. In addition to the sources already mentioned, see ILO [*1954*] and [*1948*], [*UN, 1967*]; [*Richter, 1978*]; [*Frank, 1977*]; [*Bienefeld and Godfrey, 1975*].
3. Resolution adopted at the Eighth International Conference of Labour Statisticians, Geneva, Nov–Dec., 1954. See [*Standing, 1978:30*] for a discussion on the subject.
4. An extreme case is the observance of *purdah*, or the seclusion of women, which is often seen as a 'luxury' poor women cannot afford. This attitude is found in parts of South Asia, the Middle East, North Africa and West Africa. [*Abdullah and Zeidenstein, 1978*]; [Longhurst, forthcoming].
5. See UN, [*1962*] and [*1976*]; [*Tienda, 1977*]; [*Cordell and McHale, 1975*]; [*Boulding, 1977*]; [*Denti, 1968*]; [*Safiotti, 1977*]; [*Youssef, 1977*]. Tienda, for example, elaborates the proposition that 'the proportion of female active labor varies according to indices for economic development' (p. 307) and finds that this is the case for Mexico. Yet her conclusion is based on conventional labor force statistics.
6. 'If we examine the whole process from the point of view of its results, the product, it is plain that both the instruments and the subject of labor are means of production, and that the labor itself is productive labor' [*Marx, 1967:181*].
7. The analysis of domestic work has taken place within the orthodox as well as the Marxist traditions. Typical examples of the first are compiled in Lloyd's book [*1975*], while a summary of the Marxist literature on the subject is provided by Himmelweit and Mohun [*1977*]. Subsistence production and its links with commodity production is analyzed in [*Bennholdt-Thomsen, 1978*]; [*Deere, 1977*]; and [*Wolpe, 1975*]. On the subject of reproduction see [*Edholm et al., 1976*] and [*Benería, 1979*].
8. This is so even in the much less frequent case of estimation of domestic production. Illustrations can be found in [*Walker, 1969*]; [*Scott, 1972*]; [*Vanek, 1974*].
9. In India, for example, it is clear that among the proportion of the population that have lost access to land, women are less likely than men to find wage employment [*Mies, 1978*]. As a result, unemployment figures for women are high; the Committee on the Status of Women in India estimated that, in 1971, women represented 60 per cent of rural unemployment and 56 per cent of urban unemployment (p. 160). Yet it is highly likely that these figures under-represent female unemployment because women can always take refuge in the household and move out of the conventionally defined labor force. A second example comes from Latin America where it has been estimated that in the rural areas underemployment is more than twice as high as the national unemployment rate, and that most of the unemployed are young people and married women [*ILO PREALC, 1976*].
10. '... There is a problem of specifying what is meant by "work" thus drawing a dividing line between economic and non-economic activity. The problem is an important one with respect to such activities as growing vegetables, repairing a dwelling, collecting firewood, processing food or scaring away birds' [*Turvey, 1978:8*]. A similar concern is expressed by Mueller: '... the distinction between economic activities and housework is basic to the *traditional measurement of employment*. Yet for the self-employed, and specially for people engaged in subsistence agriculture, the distinction is rather artificial. Activities that may occupy much of their time are on the borderline between economic work and housework, with the result that difficult classification and measurement problems arise.' [*Mueller, 1978:2*] (emphasis mine).
11. Although research on the subject has taken place mostly for the industrialized and more developed countries, they include a variety of countries at different levels of development and economic and political organization. Szalai's studies [*1971*], for example, refer to 12 countries, including Peru, Eastern European and Western countries. An analysis of the constancy in time spent on housework in the United States can be found in Hartmann [*1974*]. However given that these are the countries that have experienced the greatest amount of change, it is reasonable to expect that a similar situation will be found in other countries.
12. I have called this type of situation 'the paradox of Chaouen' to describe the conditions in this Northern Moroccan town where most men are idle due to the unemployment created by the replacement of traditional crafts by modern imported products; women, on the other hand, can be seen busily moving around town and in the countryside carrying on the main burden of

subsistence and family production. Yet, according to 1975 statistics for Morocco, only 15 per cent of the labor force were women [*ILO, 1977*].

REFERENCES

Abdullah, A., and Zeidenstein, S., 1978, 'Village Women of Bangladesh. Prospects for Change', Unpublished ILO study, Jan.
Anker, R., and Knowles, J., 1978, 'A Micro Analysis of Female Labor Force Participation in Africa', in Standing and Sheehan, see separate entry.
Beechey, V., 1977, 'Some Notes on Female Wage Labour in Capitalist Production', *Capital and Class*, Autumn, 45–66.
Benería, L., 1977, *Mujer, Economia y Patriarcado Durante el Periodo Franquista*, Barcelona: Anagrama.
Benería, L., 1979, 'Reproduction, Production and the Sexual Division of Labor', *Cambridge Journal of Economics*, Sept.
Benería, L., 'Accounting for Women's Work' (forthcoming).
Bennholdt-Thomsen, V., 1978, 'Subsistence Reproduction and General Reproduction', paper presented at the Conference on the Subordination of Women and the Development Process, IDS, Sept.
Bienefeld, M., and Godfrey, M., 1975, 'Measuring Unemployment and the Informal Sector. Some Conceptual and Statistical Problems', *IDS Bulletin*, Vol. 7, No. 3, Oct., 4–10.
Blanchard, F., 1979, 'Demographic Pincer Closing on Industrialized World', *ILO Information*, Vol. 15, No. 2, May.
Boserup, E., 1970, *Woman's Role in Economic Development*, London: George Allen and Unwin.
Boulding, E., 1977, *Women in the Twentieth Century World*, Sage Publications, New York: John Wiley and Sons.
Bukh, J., 1979, *The Village Woman in Ghana*, Uppsala: Scandinavian Institute of African Studies.
Committee on the Status of Women in India, 1974, *Towards Equality*, New Delhi: CSWI.
Cordell, M., and McHale, J., 1975, *Women in World Trends*, Center for Integrative Studies, State University of New York at Binghamton.
Deere, C. D., 1977, 'The Agricultural Division of Labor by Sex: Myths, Facts and Contradictions in the Northern Peruvian Sierra', paper presented at the Joint National Meeting of the Latin American Studies Association, Houston, Texas.
Deere, C. D., 1976, 'Rural Women Subsistence Production in the Capitalist Periphery', *Review of Radical Political Economics*, Vol. 8, No. 1, Spring.
Denti, E., 1968, 'Sex-Age Patterns of Labor Force Participation by Urban and Rural Populations', *International Labor Review*, Vol. 98, No. 6, Dec., 525–50.
Edholm, F., Harris, O., and Young, K., 1977, 'Conceptualizing women', *Critique of Anthropology*, Vol. 9/10, 101–30.
Fee, T., 1976, 'Domestic Labor: An Analysis of Housework and its Relation to the Production Process', *Review of Radical Political Economics*, Vol. 8, No. 1, Spring, 1–17.
Frank, W., 1977, 'The Necessity and Possibility of Comprehensive Information Systems for Agriculture', International Association of Agricultural Economists, *Members Bulletin*, No. 1, Oxford: Agricultural Economists Institute, July.
Galbraith, J. K., 1973, *Economics and the Public Purpose*, Boston: Houghton Miflin Co.
Gulati, Leela, 1975, 'Occupational Distribution of Working Women. An Inter-State Comparison', *Economic and Political Weekly*, 25 Oct., 1692–1704.
Hartmann, H., 1974, 'Capitalism and Women's Work in the Home, 1900–1930', Ph.D. dissertation, Yale University.
Himmelweit, S., and Mohun, S., 1977, 'Domestic Labour and Capital', *Cambridge Journal of Economics*, Vol. 1, Mar.
Huntington, S., 1975, 'Issues in Woman's Role in Economic Development: Critique and Alternatives', *Journal of Marriage and the Family*, Vol. 37, No. 1, 4, 1001–11.
ILO/PREALC, 1976, *The Employment Problem of Latin America, Facts, Outlooks and Policies*, Santiago.
ILO, 1976, *International Recommendations on Labor Statistics*, Geneva.
ILO, 1977, *Labor Force Projections*, Geneva.

ILO, 1978, 'Condiciones de Trabjo, Formacion Profesional y Empleo de la Mujer', report prepared for the 11th Conference of American States Members of the ILO.

League of Nations, 1938, *Statistics of the Gainfully Occupied Population. Definitions and Classifications Recommended by the Committee of Statistical Experts*, Studies and reports on Statistical Methods, No. 1, Geneva.

Lloyd, C. (ed.), 1975, *Sex, Discrimination and the Division of Labour*, New York: Columbia University Press.

Longhurst, R., 'Resource Allocation and the Sexual Division of Labour: A Case Study of a Moslem, Hausa Village in Northern Nigeria' (forthcoming).

Marx, K., 1911, *A Contribution to the Critique of Political Economy*, Chicago: Charles Kerr & Co.

Marx, K., 1967, *Capital*, Vol. 1, New York: International Publishers.

Mies, M., 1978, 'Consequences of Capitalist Penetration for Women's Subsistence Reproduction', paper read at the Seminar on Underdevelopment and Subsistence Production in South East Africa, April 1978.

Mueller, E., 1978, 'Time Use Data', Population Studies Center, University of Michigan.

Mueller, M., 'Women and Men, Power and Powerlessness in Lesotho', included in *Women and National Development*.

Reiter, R. (ed.), 1975, *Towards an Anthropology of Women*, New York: Monthly Review Press.

Richter, L., 1978, *Labor Force Information in Developing Countries*, Geneva: ILO.

Robbins, L., 1932, *The Nature and Significance of Economic Science*, London, Macmillan.

Rubbo, A., 1975, 'The Spread of Capitalism in Rural Columbia' in Reiter, see above.

Saffiotti, H., 1977, 'Women, Mode of Production, and Social Formations', *Latin American Perspectives*, Vol, IV, Nos. 1 & 2, Winter/Spring 1977, 27–37.

Scott, Ann Crittenden, 1972, 'The Value of Housework: For Love or Money?', *Ms* Magazine, July.

Seccombe, W., 1974, 'The Housewife and her Labor under Capitalism', *New Left Review*, No. 83.

Smith, A., 1975, *The Wealth of Nations*, Harmondsworth: Penguin Books.

Standing, G., 1970, 'Labour Force Participation in Historical Perspectives: Proletarianisation in Jamaica', in ILO., WEP 2–21/WP. 50.

Standing, G., 1978, *Labor Force Participation and Development*, Geneva: ILO.

Standing, G., and Sheehan, G. (eds.), 1978, *Labor Force Participation in Low Income Countries*, Geneva: ILO.

Stoler, A., 'Class Structure and Female Anatomy in Rural Java', in Wellesley Editorial Committee (ed.), *Women and National Development*, 74–88.

Sweezy, P., 1942, *The Theory of Capitalist Development*, New York: Monthly Review Press.

Szalai, A., et al., 1972, *The Use of Time*, The Hague: Mouton Press.

Tienda, M., 1977, Diferenciacion Regional y Transformacion Sectoral de la Mano de Obra Femenina en Mexico, 1970', *Demografia y Economia*, XI, 3, 307–25.

Turvey, R., 1978, 'Household Labor Statistics of the Labor Force in Developing Countries', Geneva: ILO internal circulation.

Vanek, J., 1974, 'Time Spent in Housework', *Scientific American*, Nov., 116–20.

Walker, K., 1969, 'Homemaking Still Takes Time', *Journal of Home Economics*, Vol. 61, No. 8, Oct.

Wellesley Editorial Committee (ed.), 1976, *Women and National Development: The Complexities of Change*, Chicago University Press.

Wolpe, H., 1975, 'The Theory of Internal Colonialism: The South Africa Case', in Oxaal, I., et al. (eds.), *Beyond the Sociology of Development*, London: Routledge.

Women and Agriculture in sub-Saharan Africa: Implications for Development (an Exploratory Study)

*by Judy C. Bryson** *

Data on the importance of women's role in agriculture in sub-Saharan Africa and the social structures supporting the women's role are considered to clarify the interaction between the production systems and the social systems. The results are discussed with respect to their impact on the two-sector 'agriculture-industry' development models and their implications for future development. The paper concludes that women's role in agriculture supported past development but that the failure to recognise/enhance their activities is contributing to current problems with the food supply which can be overcome most effectively by working with rather than against the women.

I. INTRODUCTION

Considerable progress has been made in the last decade in documenting the importance of female labour in food crop production (and to a lesser extent, in cash crop production) in sub-Saharan Africa. However, there is a notable gap between knowledge of the specifics of women's roles and identification of the implications of this information for agricultural transformation and overall development. With the exception of those theorists who are specifically concerned with the issues of women and development, most of the books and articles written on African agriculture by agricultural and development economists still fail to consider which policies and programmes would build most effectively on the existing division of labour in food crop production. Instead, the implicit suggestion in most of the writings is that a male takeover of the sector would result in greater progress in food crop production and overall growth, and consequently that men should be encouraged to do so at least with respect to the more profitable crops.[1]

Whether or not this attitude is correct depends upon the nature of the social and economic factors underlying women's role in food crop production and their resistance (or lack of resistance) to change. What is needed is a better understanding of how the social systems and production systems interact, and the implications of that interaction for growth in food crop production as well as overall development.

* The assistance of Phil Leeson and Diane Elson of Manchester University is acknowledged. They supervised my master's dissertation and, in the process, helped me to clarify the ideas presented in this paper. Much of the information on Cameroon used in the paper was collected in the course of a study financed by the United States Agency for International Development Mission to Cameroon, however, the opinions expressed here should be attributed to me alone.

This paper is a contribution to the subject which results from the years I spent working with and studying this issue. Eight years were spent in Ghana, and much shorter periods in Burundi and Lesotho. Another year was spent collecting and analysing information on the role of women in development in Cameroon plus a further year preparing a master's dissertation which explored the implications for development of women's role in agriculture in Cameroon. The Cameroon data indicate that the women's role in agriculture has profound implications for the development of the country, and the similarities between the situation in Cameroon and the conditions I observed in other countries of sub-Saharan Africa convinced me that the findings have much wider applicability.

The present paper considers information available on the predominance of female labour in food crop production in sub-Saharan Africa to establish the overall importance of women in agriculture in this area. The results of that study are presented in the next section of this paper and demonstrate the striking differences between sub-Saharan Africa and the rest of the world with respect to the importance of female labour in agriculture which holds for intensive as well as extensive agricultural systems. General background reading of the anthropological literature on African societies and the results of the colonial experience also show that the various countries in sub-Saharan Africa share many features in common. The third section of the paper describes the social structures supporting the predominance of female labour in agriculture, followed by a discussion of the effects of changes in the economic production systems in the twentieth century. In the final sections the implications of this information for agricultural production and economic development will be discussed.

Throughout the paper, most of the specific examples provided will be drawn from Cameroon as I have the most detailed knowledge of the situation in that country. It is recognised that this paper represents an introductory study only, and that the overall situation in sub-Saharan Africa is both more complicated and more various than can be presented here. I hope other researchers will be stimulated to test the ideas presented in this paper against their own experience and suggest additional perspectives. The problems of food shortages in Africa which result from the failure to stimulate and assist farmers to produce more food is one of the most significant development problems facing the world today, and needs much more attention to produce solutions which are in keeping with African culture.

II. THE PREDOMINANCE OF FEMALE LABOUR IN FOOD CROP PRODUCTION

Women in sub-Saharan Africa have a predominant role in agricultural production; a fact which has been substantiated by a number of investigators. One of the pioneering efforts at synthesis of the information is contained in Ester Boserup's book, *Woman's Role in Economic Development*. Boserup reviewed studies which had been made in African villages (most of which were carried out in the 1950s and 1960s) and found that, in general, more women than men in cultivator families were doing agricultural work, and the women were usually working more hours per week in agriculture than the men. As a result, in almost all the cases, women 'were found to do around 70 per cent and in one case nearly 80 per cent of the total'. [*Boserup, 1970:22*] It should be noted that Boserup was considering total agricultural production, including cash crops where men are more heavily involved.

As it is possible that the studies Boserup and others have publicised represent special cases, I made a study of data contained in the 'Ethnographic Atlas' [*Murdock, 1967:109–236*], one of the most comprehensive listings available of data which have been collected on the cultures of the world. A wide variety of information is available on each society included in the 'Ethnographic Atlas', among which are data on the importance of agriculture in subsistence, the type of agriculture and the division of labour in production.

Analysis of this data confirms the fact that the cases presented by investigators such as Boserup represent a general phenomenon in sub-Saharan Africa. In addition, it indicates that the importance of female labour in agriculture in the region is quite different from the overall importance of female labour in agriculture world-wide (summarised in Table 1 below). The data on sub-Saharan Africa included in Table 1 is based on a random, independent sample of sub-Sahara African societies which I drew from the 'Ethnographic Atlas'. The distribution of labour found in that sample is compared to the distribution of labour which appeared in the world-wide samples of horticultural and agricultural societies drawn from the same data base by M. Kay Martin and Barbara Voorhies [*Martin and Voorhies, 1975:283*]. As the Martin and Voorhies data includes sub-Saharan Africa, it is to be expected that the differences would be even more striking if the sub-Sahara African data were to be removed from their sample.

TABLE 1

| Area | Division of Labour | | | |
	Male Predominance	Female Predominance	Equal Participation	Total
Sub-Sahara Africa	10 (19%)	27 (52%)	15 (29%)	52 (100%)
World	92 (47%)	67 (34%)	38 (19%)	197 (100%)

A number of anthropological writers have pointed out that the importance of female labour in production tends to be lower in societies which have intensive agricultural systems (intensive systems employ techniques such as ploughing, irrigation or cultivation practices such as crop rotation and fertilisation to achieve higher yields per unit of land) than in extensive cultivation systems. The Martin and Voorhies data provide an illustration of this proposition as the aggregate data presented above was based on two separate samples drawn from the 'Ethnographic Atlas', one for 'horticultural' societies and one for 'agricultural' societies ('horticultural' was the term they applied to extensive cultivation systems and 'agricultural' to systems which used one or more of the forms of intensification mentioned above). The results of these two samples are shown separately in Table 2.

As the agricultural systems of sub-Saharan Africa tend to be extensive cultivation systems, a simplistic application of this information could lead analysts to assume that the introduction of modern, intensive agricultural techniques

TABLE 2

Type of Cultivation System	Division of Labour			
	Male Predominance	Female Predominance	Equal Participation	Total
Horticulture	17 (17%)	52 (50%)	35 (33%)	104 (100%)
Agriculture	75 (81%)	15 (16%)	3 (3%)	93 (100%)

would result in the displacement of women from agricultural production. An early example is provided by Lord Lugard's expectation as to the consequences of the introduction of oxen ploughs in Kenya for he observed, 'Since men alone tend oxen in Africa, the result, as I have elsewhere said, will be to replace female labour in the fields to a large extent.' [*Lugard, 1965:517*]. The passing of years and the continuing importance of women in agriculture in Kenya have proved Lord Lugard to be wrong, and demonstrates the lack of validity of this attitude. However, it is useful to examine the situation in sub-Sahara African agriculture more closely, as the idea that female labour will be displaced by the intensification and modernisation of agriculture is implicit in much of the current writing on agricultural development in the region.

In an article on women's labour in Africa which was primarily concerned with sub-Saharan Africa, Jack Goody and Joan Buckley showed a similar result to that of Martin and Voorhies. Goody and Buckley prepared an analysis of the entire population of African societies, including North Africa, contained in the 'Ethnographic Atlas' with respect to the division of labour in extensive versus intensive cultivation systems. Their analysis demonstrated that the predominance of female labour in production fell from 80 per cent in the extensive cultivation systems to 20 per cent in intensive cultivation systems. They performed a x_2 significance test on their information and found that the difference in the division of labour was significant at the .001 level [*Goody and Buckley, 1973:110*]. However, their result is not based on an independent random sample, but on the entire population of African societies contained in the 'Ethnographic Atlas', and as George Murdock emphasises in his introduction to the 'Ethnographic Atlas' such a sample is not suitable for statistical tests.[2]

The independent random sample of sub-Sahara African societies which I drew from the 'Ethnographic Atlas' had a very different result from that presented by Goody and Buckley. The prominence of extensive cultivation systems is shown by the sample; 42 out of 52 societies are in that classification. However, further analysis of the sample shows that while female labour is reduced somewhat in importance in intensive cultivation systems, there is no significant difference between the labour usage practices of societies having extensive cultivation systems as compared to those with intensive cultivation systems.[3] These results are summarised in Table 3.

The results shown in Tables 2 and 3 indicate that the difference between the importance of female labour in agriculture in sub-Saharan Africa as compared to the situation on a world-wide basis is maintained even with respect to the labour usage patterns of intensive agricultural systems. The reasons for this difference must be sought in factors other than technology, and an important part of the

TABLE 3

Type of Cultivation System – Sub-Sahara Africa	Division of Labour						
	Male Predominance		Female Predominance		Equal Participation		Total
Extensive	8	(19%)	23	(55%)	11	(26%)	42 (100%)
Intensive	2	(20%)	4	(40%)	4	(40%)	10 (100%)

answer is provided by the social structures which are discussed in the next section of the paper.

III. SOCIAL STRUCTURES SUPPORTING THE DIVISION OF LABOUR IN AGRICULTURE

This section considers basic questions concerning the organisation of agricultural production including: (1) what are the means of acquiring land for farming?; (2) what are the social imperatives sustaining the predominant role of women in food crop production? Although much of the material discussed below may be familiar to some readers, it is generally available only in scattered references. Accordingly, it is believed that a systematic outline directly relating social structures to the production systems will help to clarify the situation and provide a basis for evaluating the final analytical sections.

Until recently, population densities in sub-Saharan Africa have been low, and land has not been in short supply in most places; as a result, individual ownership of particular plots of land has not been common. This situation is changing, particularly with respect to land used for the production of export and industrial crops ('cash crops') where ownership is becoming more individualised; in addition, land registration has been introduced in some areas, for instance, Kenya. [*Anthony, et. al., 1979:20*]. However, the following account is still generally true for land used to produce food crops.

Social groups, which may be extended families, lineages composed of persons related through either the male or female line, or larger groups such as tribes, control areas of land. The right to use land within the area depends on membership in the group, and decisions on allocation are made by the family elders or lineage heads. In some traditional political systems, chiefs or kings are said to own the land, but the authority to decide on allocations to individuals is usually delegated to the lineage or household heads.

As these are usually males, whether a woman comes from a matrilineal or patrilineal society, her access to at least a portion of the land she farms is generally dependent on her husband (or his lineage group), or on the males of her lineage group. However, in some social groups, the woman's mother or other female relatives may also have the right to allocate land they have farmed to her,[4] and it is sometimes also possible for a woman to borrow land from other individuals or to clear and claim unused land for her own. As a result, a woman's access to this basic productive resource is generally not a problem, and it can be said that women have more control over land in sub-Saharan Africa than they do in most other parts of the world.

When land registration systems have been introduced however, either in the context of resettlement schemes, or consolidation and registration schemes such as those in Kenya, the rights of female users have tended to be ignored and the male ownership rights stressed. As land law in Africa is undergoing rapid development and governments are moving to formalise or change customary law [*Hellen, 1977:55–73*], women's future position in this regard is likely to be much worse than at present, particularly if the importance of their role in agriculture continues to be ignored.

An important point to emphasise is that most of the land allocated for farming is given to married couples; whether or not the wife plays a predominant role in agriculture, a man must be married before he is socially considered to be an adult. Until then, he has the right to be fed by his mother, and as far as the society is concerned, has no need for land of his own. This fact helps to explain the lack of interest in returning to the land which is observed among unemployed single males in urban areas. The situation of single women is somewhat different; they may be allocated plots to farm by their families as part of their apprenticeship, and may farm actively, especially if they have any children. Widowed and divorced women generally also have access to farming land to provide their own subsistence, and that of their minor children in the case of widows and divorced women in matrilineal systems (in patrilineal systems, divorced women have to leave their children with the husband's family).

Marriage is normally preceded by the payment of bridewealth from the family of the husband to that of the wife. In the past, this was in the form of valuable gifts (socially prestigious items: goats, cows, cowrie shells, beads, etc., depending on the group) or sometimes 'bride service' where the fiancé worked for the family of the future wife for a certain period. In more recent times, bridewealth has been translated more often into money terms. Bridewealth has often been misunderstood by outside observers, who view it as an enslavement of women, i.e. that women are being bought and sold. However, the girl is not available to everyone but only to suitors whom her family consider acceptable. In addition, the girl's family have to be prepared to return the goods if the marriage breaks up through the wife's misconduct or if she leaves her husband without good cause. The proceeds of the transaction are generally used to secure a wife for some member of the girl's family, so in effect, a person is replaced by a person. In patrilineal systems, payment of the bridewealth is essential if the children of the union are to be members of the husband's family.

Monetisation of the bridewealth has had a number of effects on the situation of women, most of which are negative (due to the fact that payment of the bridewealth in cash more closely approximates a commercial transaction). However, one interesting consequence of the monetisation of the bridewealth and the new economic activities introduced in the colonial era, which are discussed below, is the possibility presented to women in securing their independence from their husbands. If a woman can repay the bridewealth herself, she is free to leave her marriage without upsetting her natal family.

In the past, there was little likelihood that women could amass the necessary commodities themselves, but it became possible once the bridewealth was monetised and markets created for the food crops produced by the women. Male fears of this possibility have led to attempts either to increase the bridewealth, or to appropriate any funds earned by the women (although the men have generally had limited success in this regard). This fear is also a factor in male hostility to development projects whose objective is to increase the production and commercialisation of foodstuffs, or in their supplanting women in the production and sales activities connected with such projects even when women are the principal producers of food crops in the area.

Despite their marriage, both the husband and wife remain members of their own lineages; even in those patrilineal systems where it is an ideal for women to be incorporated into their husbands' families, women still retain certain links with their natal family (for instance, divorced women return to their fathers' or brothers' homes). In this situation, a woman's link with her husband's family does not become strong until she has borne children who are lineage members. Even then, many of a woman's ties and often her access to productive resources are provided by her natal family, and this is an important factor in the fragmented nature of both the patterns of holding and use of economic resources. In many societies, it is expected (and accepted by the husband) that the wife will make gifts regularly to members of her family, and help them financially in times of need.

Another reason for the often distant relationship between husband and wife and the separation of their property and incomes, is the high rate of polygynous marriages. Polygyny is an ideal for most African males, and many attain it for at least some period of their lives. Despite this fact, the incidence of polygyny at any one time rarely exceeds 35 per cent of married men, and most polygynous men have only two or at most three wives [Dorjahn, 1965:104–105]. A woman recognises, however, that what she may hope will be a monogamous marriage can be used by her husband as the first step to a polygynous marriage. Women in all marriages are concerned to keep their property clearly separate in anticipation of the problems which could result from the arrival of a co-wife.

Contrary to popular opinion, the incidence and intensity of polygyny in sub-Saharan Africa is not made possible by a large excess of females over males as the sex ratio is approximately in equilibrium with just slightly more females than males. Polygyny is thus achieved mainly by an early age at first marriage for females coupled with a relatively late age for males which increases the pool of women available for marriageable males [Dorjahn, 1965:105–109]. Marriage instability and early widowhood (due to the large differences in ages of husband and wife at first marriage) are secondary factors which help to make polygyny possible. As women often make several marriages in a lifetime, their movement from husband to husband makes it possible for more males to be polygynous, if only for a brief period of their lives.

A formal relationship between husbands and wives in polygynous marriages is necessary to avoid jealousies and quarrels between co-wives, and the relationship between co-wives is also formalised. In addition, the need to avoid quarrels creates a distant relationship between fathers and children; if the father was seen to have a closer relationship with some children than with others, it would lead to quarrels among their mothers. Conversely, there is a close relationship between mothers and their children. Among many groups there is no concept of a family as consisting of a husband, wife and children. Instead, a woman and her children constitute a clearly separate unit within the polygynous compound, and it is common for them to live in a separate residence within the compound (in matrilineal systems they may live in a different compound as the husband and wife may continue to live with their respective matrikin).

The prevalence of polygyny in sub-Saharan Africa is related to the cultivation system and land use practices. The more wives a man has, the more land he is allocated to cultivate, thus increasing his wealth and power. This is true whether or not men 'own' the crops which are produced on the land as the availability of land for their sons' families-to-be is important in keeping the allegiance and support of these young men. In addition, even when women are considered to 'own' the crops, each wife generally is required to give a portion of the harvest to her husband for his own use. Obviously, the predominant role of women in agricultural production is essential to the attractions of polygyny in this regard. It would be of little use to the man to be allocated a larger acreage of land if his labour alone was to be used to exploit it, as he might not be physically capable of realising its potential, and if he failed to farm it regularly, he could lose his usage rights to it.

The husband is usually expected to provide his wife with farming land, though land might be provided by the wife's own lineage as was noted above. As men who have several wives often decide how much land to allocate to each wife, and sometimes can reallocate the land they receive from their lineage among them, the amount of land women receive from their own kin often creates considerable differences between the independence of wives of the same man and between their ability to feed themselves and their children or to generate a marketable surplus.

In addition to providing the land, husbands normally make some input into the food production process, and most often provide assistance in clearing the land. However, evidence from Cameroon suggests that as the new economic activities of men (discussed below) take up more time than the men previously spent in agriculture, many have ceased to perform at least a portion of their other agricultural work even when the work peaks do not clash. As a result, women are cultivating smaller fields more intensively, and they may also use some of the money earned from food crop sales to hire male labour for land clearing (or husbands may provide the funds for this expense).

Husbands are expected to provide each wife with a separate kitchen which is used for a variety of social and practical purposes. In addition to cooking there, the wife uses it to store her crops, entertain her friends; and she and her children may sleep there. Her kitchen is a woman's sphere of autonomy; usually no one may enter it without her permission. In modern times, as polygyny is less prevalent, the kitchen may be replaced by a separate residence for husband and wife away from the patrilineal or matrilineal home. However, modern houseplans among the Bassa in Cameroon for example show the kitchen of the house as a room without an inside entrance which includes a bed, indicating the continuing importance to the woman of a separate room [*Champaud, 1973:24*]. Finally, a husband may provide certain other household necessities, e.g. oil, meat, cloth, and he may be expected to provide the funds for school fees (wives generally help with this expense if they have a cash income). The husband also saves his income to make capital expenditures for such items as bridewealth payments and roofing sheets for housing. Such expenses often require a man to save most of his income over a number of years in order to amass the necessary funds.

Wives on their part are expected to perform most domestic and child care duties, and also to provide a substantial portion of their own and their children's livelihood. This is true even when they do not predominate in food crop production, which explains the long list of productive activities engaged in by women which are found in the anthropological literature. The most famous of these is trading, especially among women in West Africa. Although women save some of the funds earned from these activities, they spend most of their incomes immediately on household needs, and often have to make up deficiencies in what their husbands provide them.

Part of the explanation for the importance of women in providing sustenance for the family is the prevalence among Africans of a particular concept of the child-bearing role of women. There is a general association world-wide between the 'mother' and the 'giver of food'. In Africa, the giving of food is closely allied to its production, and is often seen as an integral part of motherhood.

Success at both child bearing and food production is essential to women. In the view of society, and especially in the eyes of the women themselves, child bearing is basic to their reason for living, the very essence of their femaleness, and raising food to feed the children is part of their nurturing role. To fail in this realm would be to fail as a mother and as a person. Under these conditions, food crop production can be seen as 'women's work' *par excellence*, and men would be understandably reluctant to take it over. As Theresa Ndongko points out, a 'man performing a duty which is looked upon as that of a female is ridiculed as is a woman who performs labour assigned to males' [*Ndongko, 1976:147*].

It also must be emphasised that women take considerable pride in their agricultural work and derive personal satisfaction from their productivity. Unfortunately, most of those who have written about the women's agricultural activities have either emphasised the back-breaking nature of their toil and the observer's desire to get the women out of the hot sun and into their houses, or decried the fact that women have been left behind in the traditional sector while men have moved on to modern occupations. Both approaches ignore the wishes and attitudes of the women toward their work.

The Tikar women Phyllis Kaberry studied in the 1940s in what was then West Cameroon were very clear about the importance of what they did and their personal worth. When Kaberry asked a woman why women were mourned for four days and men for only three, she replied:

> A woman is an important thing. A man is a worthless thing indeed, because a woman gives birth to the people of the country. What work can a man do? A woman bears a child, then takes a hoe, goes to the field, and is working there; she feeds the child [with the work] there. A man only buys palm oil. Men only build houses. [*Kaberry, 1952:150*]

A recent example of the women's attitude towards their work from my own experience was the reply a sociologist working on the design of a peat project in Burundi received from the wife of one of the men working on the peat bogs. The sociologist had asked whether the woman felt that women should be employed on the bog, which is the principal source of wage income in the area (the women are not employed on the bog as a matter of policy). The woman asked, 'Who would farm?' and then went on to say that even if both she and her husband were employed on the bog, their joint income would not compensate the family for the loss of her agricultural production.

In summary, family structure and inheritance systems in sub-Saharan Africa have combined to create agricultural production systems which are very different from those found in most other parts of the world. As a result, it is difficult to apply the models of land tenure usually found in the literature on agriculture, e.g. landlord/tenant, owner-operator. The use of the household as the basic unit of analysis, with the management role assumed to be taken by the husband, and the wives filling the role of labourers under his direction, is also problematic. The presence of the wife and her competence in agricultural work are crucial to the husband, but there is considerable variation in the husband's decision-making role over her activities. Even in societies where men are closely involved in agriculture, women generally maintain an area of autonomy, e.g. special crops which they alone grow. This is essential to the women, both to meet household requirements not provided by their husbands and to fulfil their obligations to their natal families.

It is important to emphasise that the strength of the social institutions outlined above has been maintained to the present day despite the many changes which the colonial and post-colonial eras have brought to Africa. Many studies have confirmed for example, that bridewealth continues to be considered an integral part of marriage by girls and their families, and that polygyny is still a prevalent institution even among the educated urban elites. The high economic participation rates registered by women is further evidence of their continuing need to provide for themselves and their children.

IV. THE EFFECTS OF ECONOMIC CHANGE IN THE TWENTIETH CENTURY

In the conditions imposed by African social systems, it is to be expected that women's responsibilities for providing their family's food supply would not be eliminated by male productive activities whether these were inside or outside agriculture. However, the colonial experience in sub-Saharan Africa did not create conditions which forced a change-over in the division of labour in food crop production despite the rhetoric of many colonial administrators and missionaries who believed that the movement of women out of food crop production would be a positive change. Instead, female labour became more rather than less important in food crop production as males took up the new economic opportunities which were provided by the colonial system.

Male movement into new roles was to a certain extent inevitable; the colonialists had pre-empted many of their former responsibilities (administration and policing for example), and in turn, offered or required performance of new roles which involved absence from the village, e.g. portage duties or labour on roads and railroads. The demands on male labour helped to ensure that women would continue to dominate food crop production both to guarantee the food supply and to protect family rights to property in accordance with inheritance and land tenure customs.

Also important, however, were European attitudes to education for Africans, and employment provided in supporting roles in commercial ventures and the colonial administration, as the Europeans decreed that these were to be primarily for males. In addition, most European efforts in the agricultural sector were concentrated in cash crop production where men were taught by other men to grow crops such as coffee and cocoa, and were provided with considerable support and incentives. Although men were exhorted to take over food crop production as well, little assistance was given to them in this area. As they did not have the competence of women in growing food crops, and no personal inclination to acquire it, male movement into food crop production was limited.

However, the growth of urban centres associated with government, industry and foreign trade which was one of the consequences of the colonial system did help women to earn a cash income also, as it created a demand for the sale of food crops. In some cases markets were initially created by decree, but in general, women were not slow to respond to the opportunities which were created by this outlet for their produce. The women were able to consolidate their position as food sellers largely because men had new opportunities and considered food crops 'women's work' and the incomes to be derived from them less attractive than the alternatives open to the men. Women were able to dispose of most of the money they earned themselves both because their husbands knew that most was spent immediately on household needs and also because men considered the women's earnings to be small in comparison to their own.

This is no longer entirely true as some researchers have found that the small, regular amounts earned by women through sales of food produce, annually amount to half or more of the lump sums earned by their husbands when they make once yearly sales of export crops such as coffee or cocoa. [*Guyer, 1977:73*]. The increased status their earning power has given women is indicated by the controversies over bridewealth mentioned above. Women's earnings are correlated with a better standard of living for their families as well, and the fact that they spend most of what they earn immediately is an important source of rural demand for both food products and the type of industrial products which can most easily be produced in the developing countries, e.g. soap and matches.

The large numbers of men now working outside food crop production is illustrated by census data such as that collected in Cameroon in 1976 which included information on the economically active population. That census showed that 35 per cent of economically active males were involved in employment outside agriculture, and a further 22 per cent were involved in export crop production (these figures are taken from preliminary data on the census which were supplied to me by the Direction de la Statistique, Yaounde, Cameroon). Accordingly, more than 50 per cent of adult males are not involved in subsistence production. On the other hand, despite the importance of food sales to women, data on sales of food crops from the same country indicate that they amount to only 25 per cent of total production.

This illustration points up another difference between the experience of Cameroon and that of other parts of the world, as it is generally considered that the involvement of a majority of adult males with productive activities other than food production is characteristic of the economic stage of 'indirect agricultural consumption', i.e. 'the whole non-agricultural population and at least part of the agricultural population satisfy their needs through a market in which farm goods are sold'. [*Van-Bath, 1963:23–5*]. However, in this instance, rural women are still providing the family food supply (and most of the food crops marketed) regardless of their husbands' activities.

Further consideration of the Cameroon data also suggests the physical impossibility of a male take-over of food crop production given the numerical importance of women in this sector. Women provide 61 per cent of the labour force in food crop production (84 per cent of economically active women are in food crop production) while unemployed males in Cameroon amount to less than 50 per cent of the female labour force (these figures are also derived from the preliminary census data). Further, many of the unemployed males are young and urban based. They have not been trained in food crop production and will not have access to land through their families until they are married. Clearly, any major new involvement by males would require transferring them from their present occupations which would create labour shortages in other sectors.

Accordingly, the experience of Cameroon suggests that the role of women in food crop production is a structural fact in the production systems in sub-Saharan Africa which cannot be changed easily either from a social or an economic point of view. The development implications of these conditions will be considered in the final sections, first in the context of a two-sector 'agriculture-industry' division of the economy, and then with respect to the implications for future development.

V. THE DEVELOPMENT PROCESS — 'AGRICULTURE-INDUSTRY'

In the conditions which result from women's involvement in agriculture in sub-Saharan Africa, it could be said that a two sector division of the economy into agriculture and industry becomes almost a two sex division. This is especially true if the sectorisation chosen places modern manufacturing and production of export crops in the 'industrial' sector and includes all other economic activities in 'agriculture'. Women are producing the food, and are heavily involved also in the marketing activities. As a result, the difficulties involved in assuring that the food supply is protected while male labour is drawn off into new economic activities are minimised.

In addition, it has not been necessary to pay full world market prices to induce men to take up production of export crops, as these activities do not have to provide sufficient return to meet the men's subsistence costs (and those of their 'dependents'). The 'export tax' on these crops, which amounts to the difference between the price paid to producers (plus expenses) and the price secured by the government in world markets, was an important source of revenue for the colonial government, just as it is for the independent governments. These funds have been used to build up an infrastructure of roads, railroads, power and communications as well as to finance the education system, development projects, etc.

Thus, the fact that men are involved in food production in only a minor way in a majority of societies makes it easier to squeeze the agricultural sector to finance the development of agriculture and other sectors, as the 'opportunity cost' of the men's new activities is very low. In addition, it has been possible to invest funds to produce capital outside agriculture to a much greater extent than would be possible if men had a more important role in food crop production. It would be necessary, for instance, to increase the efficiency of food crop production substantially if the men were required to produce the food *and* provide the labour force for the new economic activities. Such a change would require capital funds to pay for both research and improved inputs. Instead sufficient production has been generated to meet the demand resulting from population growth and the higher incomes of industrial workers, primarily by increasing labour inputs on the part of women (and to a lesser extent by increasing efficiency in production on the part of women) ás will be discussed below.

However, while the women have helped to make it possible to mobilise the 'hidden savings potential' of the agriculture sector, they also benefit from the establishment of new productive activities as these result in a demand for the sale of food crops (due to the growth of urban centres): although the women continue to provide the subsistence of the producers of export/industrial crops and industrial/commercial workers (their male relatives), once markets are established, the women can both meet the subsistence needs of urban workers and increase their own consumption by selling food crops in the markets and using the income derived from the sales to purchase new industrial products whether home produced or imported (and also semi-processed or fresh local food stuffs). However, this circumstance does not alter the fact that the women's situation is still far from acceptable, or that they have to work relatively longer hours for lower earning than do the men.

As most production systems have not been mechanised and still use traditional inputs and techniques, one would expect that the production gains per worker registered in the agriculture sector over the last fifty years have been achieved primarily by additional labour inputs (the suggestion that labour slack exists in the traditional agriculture sector for whatever reason is important to the successful operation of the 'agriculture-industry' development models). An indication that this has occurred in some places is provided by data which compare the pre-colonial and post-colonial situation of the Pahouin women in the forest area of Cameroon. The data should be treated with caution, however, as the hours worked by any particular woman vary greatly depending on the number of persons she is supporting, her age, the ages of her children, her work habits, etc.

P. Laburthe-Tolra collected information from elderly Beti women on their activities in the early years of the twentieth century which suggests that their working week averaged 45 hours. This total was divided between 32 hours of domestic labour and thirteen hours of field work. In times of peak agricultural work, the total was closer to 59 hours per week and at other times dropped to essentially the 32 hours of domestic work [*Laburthe-Tolra, 1975:652*].

Jane Guyer's research in 1975–6 into the situation of women in the same tribal group suggests that the average time spent on the agricultural work necessary to provide subsistence for the family now totals 21 hours per week. However, Guyer's study also shows the impact of opportunities for the sale of food crops as it is a comparative analysis of the activities of women in two villages, Nkometou which is on the main Yaounde/Obala road (one of the most travelled routes in Cameroon), while the second village, Nkolfeb is a three-four kilometre walk from the Yaounde/Okola road which was unpaved and in poor condition.

In Nkometou, women had a choice of outlets for their produce; the outlets were within easy reach and compatible with the social and physical constraints on the women's activities. The situation in Nkolfeb was very different and the women's marketing activities were accomplished with great difficulty. These differences were reflected in the working patterns as the Nkolfeb women worked only three hours a week producing for the market. In Nkometou, however, women were working around ten hours per week above the amount required for subsistence, a total of 31 hours a week in the fields. These are average figures, and the Nkometou average suggests labour peak requirements of approximately 50 hours of work per week in agriculture alone.

The extra workload of the Nkometou women is spread throughout the year, and derived from working a larger main plot in the first growing season, and planting small fields in speciality crops whose labour requirements did not conflict with that of the main field. The extra eight hours a week worked for subsistence production by all women over the hours worked in the early part of the century probably compensates both for the withdrawal of male support and concomitant changes in the production system (e.g. the disappearance of yam fields where men helped to build the necessary mounds and their replacement by cassava which is tended entirely by women) [Guyer, 1977:49–53].

Although these working hours are still supportable, they are daunting when combined with the women's domestic responsibilities. Guyer states that these take more than six hours per day (including collection of water, firewood and food preparation) [Guyer, 1977:49]. This suggests an average working week of 73 hours in Nkometou and a much higher peak figure. In the latter instance, however, one would expect that the women would shortcut certain of their household duties. These figures suggest that the time required for domestic labour has also increased substantially, possibly due to the loss of assistance from other females; the numbers of co-wives have fallen and daughters are now likely to be attending school.

The question of the women's workload is a serious one, both because the additional agricultural output necessary to keep up with population growth and increasing rates of urbanisation will require further inputs of time on their part in all likelihood, but also because the heavy burden of work may be harmful to the women and their children (especially those under five who require regular attention). However, it should be emphasised that while the women and their families might benefit from shorter working hours for women, this does not mean that women necessarily have to leave their productive roles. Assistance in increasing the efficiency of their agricultural work and/or assistance with their domestic responsibilities could have the same effect, and would result in improvements without lowering incomes.

Such a process apparently took place among the Luo in Kenya between 1930–1945 and included both changes within agriculture (the introduction of oxen ploughing, changes in crop mix) and changes in methods of food processing. The extra time gained by women through these innovations was invested in trade [Hay, 1976:106–7]. While it is likely that the total working day of the Luo women has not really been reduced, the experience of tribes like the Luo should be studied to determine if they are replicable in other locations.

VI. IMPLICATIONS FOR FUTURE DEVELOPMENT

Despite the success registered in increasing the productivity of the agriculture sector in sub-Saharan Africa in the twentieth century, signs of stress have been accumulating in recent years. Many areas have experienced periods of acute food shortages; chronic problems are indicated by data which indicate that at least half of the countries in the area have lower per capita food availabilities in the late 1970s than they did a decade earlier, and some have significantly less [*The World Bank, 1979:126–7*].

Although various ·groups have been blamed for the situation, most analysts agree that the main source of the problems is the failure to reach rural food producers with effective programmes for increasing production. Although further production response could be expected to result from improved market integration, it is highly likely that any substantial progress will require significant changes in technology and improved inputs in the production process.

Allied to the production problem is a demand problem – while urban demand may be sufficient to make technological change in production possible and profitable in areas immediately adjacent to the cities, transformation of the rural sector must depend upon the growth of demand among the producers themselves. Kenneth Anthony *et al.* analysed the possible markets for foodstuffs in Africa and came to the conclusion that

> any sizable increase in agricultural production for domestic sale must look for its market among consumers who already have or will substitute purchased foodstuffs for those they grow themselves and who will increase the amount they spend on food purchases as their incomes grow. [*Anthony, 1979:102*].

It is suggested here that the solution to the demand problem depends critically on the female food producers. The majority of rural men do not consider themselves responsible for assuring the family's food supply; accordingly, increased food crop production and marketings by men will not lead to early and substantial increases in rural market demand for food. The men will spend most of their incomes on other items and family food needs will continue to be met primarily by women's subsistence production. Demand growth will be further restricted by the drop in the women's incomes as men take over production for the urban market and other problems are likely to occur with respect to the rural standard of living.

For example, if men were to take over more of the farming land to produce speciality crops for urban markets, the problems of feeding rural families could increase. Even if part of what the men produce is consumed by their families, it is unlikely that the men will produce the broad range of crops required for a balanced family diet. However, their increased land demands will restrict the land available to women to meet these needs; at a minimum, women could be assigned fields further away from their homes, thus increasing the burdens and time involved in farming.

It is not suggested that transformation of the agricultural sector will never occur if programmes concentrate only on males, and the problems which could arise with respect to rural diets if women's access to land is restricted would be one factor forcing change to occur. What is suggested is that change will come about much more slowly as each adjustment comes up against social expectations concerning women's contribution to the family. On the other hand, as women are responsible for the food supply, if means can be found to increase their incomes, they will be encouraged to specialise, and to buy the rest of their requirements thus creating a larger market for food products.

The current situation in agriculture in which women have been able to maintain and improve their position has arisen largely because men specialised in other areas with greater income opportunities. If the women's position is to be protected (and it is argued here that this is essential to rapid change) development efforts should concentrate on ensuring that the men continue to have sufficiently attractive options, e.g. programmes which attempt to improve the activities of smallholder producers of export and industrial crops are preferable to investments in large scale plantations. Small-scale industrial development located in rural areas as opposed to concentration of production in large units in the cities is another example of a helpful approach.

If men are involved in a mix of activities, it is likely that women will both be able to command sufficient land to meet family needs and sufficient independence to control the incomes derived from food crop sales. If men's activities are sufficiently profitable, they will be less concerned also about the rising incomes of the women. Indeed, in these conditions, separate and growing success in both men's and women's activities could lead to mutually reinforcing benefits, with men demanding and receiving a fairer share of the value of the export and industrial crops they produce, and women seeking to maintain their position by working to increase their income in line with the men. As this strategy would increase income and hence demand for the products produced by both industry and agriculture, it would benefit the entire economy.

The design of programmes to enhance the women's productivity would have to be carefully handled. It is important to avoid presenting them as commercial programmes as that would defeat their purpose, i.e. 'cash' crops are male crops and men would be more likely to take over such programmes. It is suggested here that the best approach would be to use a female extension staff with the stated purpose of improving the family's food supply, while making efforts to ensure that the women have ready access to markets in order to dispose of any surplus. In this regard, the benefits to be derived from improved food processing and storage should not be overlooked, as this would have the same effect as increased production of the basic product (as well as anticipating solutions to the 'second generation' problems of increased agricultural production). Processing is also in the women's sphere of responsibility, and extension of improved techniques is within the competence of many of the existing home science extension personnel.

The time constraints on women are also important as it is likely that they may not be able to meet the labour demands of all these increased activities themselves. The success of women in retaining control of production will probably depend on whether the men's involvement can be restricted to a few labour peaks and especially to the areas where women's involvement has always been limited, e.g. land clearing. If this can be done, women could hire male labour for this task, and pay their husbands to organise the work crews in the same way that wives are paid when they assist in export crop harvests. On the other hand, weeding has been primarily the responsibility of women, and efforts to lessen the burden of weeding (which can be expected to become an even heavier charge if fertiliser is used) would be particularly helpful to the women in meeting the expanded requirements for their own labour. Studies of the crop production systems should be made with these constraints in mind, (and take into account the experience of groups such as the Luo discussed above) so that solutions can be found within the women's management capabilities.

Although the problems are complicated, they are no more complicated than those that arise from programmes which attempt to force change in opposition to social institutions. A development path which builds on women's traditional role in agriculture is only one of the options open to the nations of sub-Saharan Africa. However, development which makes use of the potential benefits to be derived from enhancing the women's activities has the best prospect of rapid and sustainable success. Other approaches will have less success and a problematic impact on rural standards of living. In sum, they represent a denial of African potential and African culture.

NOTES

1. An example of this attitude is contained in the recent book by Kenneth Anthony, *et al.*, 'Sex linked roles pose problems in the [economic] transformation ... [however] New crops that have been adopted into the farming system have often led to modifications of the traditional definitions of "male" and "female" crops when their economic potential was large. Cultivation of food crops is no longer exclusively a woman's activity in those parts of Africa where the domestic demand for staple food has led to increasing commercialization.' [*Anthony, et al., 1979:118*].
2. Murdock studied the problems of using the 'Ethnographic Atlas' for statistical research, and proposed techniques for achieving valid results. Many cultures are closely related, and Murdock proposed grouping them into cultural clusters. He divides sub-Saharan Africa into 85 cultural clusters; examples from all clusters are included in the 'Ethnographic Atlas'. However, two societies from the same cluster would not be independent of each other, and in addition, some clusters have been studied more exhaustively than others, so if the entire population in the 'Ethnographic Atlas' is used, the results will be biased. Only one representative from each cultural cluster should be used, and that society should be selected by random techniques. In addition, cultures which are close together may not be independent (i.e. they may have borrowed cultural features from each other) so Murdock proposes a 'three degree rule': all societies included in the sample must be at least three degrees latitude or three degrees longitude from each other. Murdock's rules for obtaining a valid statistical sample are summarised [*Murdock, 1967:114*] and were followed to obtain my own sample of sub-Sahara African societies.
3. A x_2 significance test performed on the data yielded a value of 0.88 which does not fall into the critical region even at the 0.50 level.
4. The difference between the rights of the women and that of the inheritors of the land is that the women's rights are weaker rights, and can be overridden in certain cases, e.g. as female usage rights are passed on to women who are progressively more distantly related to the inheritors, an inheritor could get the land back, especially at the time it is being given to a new user.

REFERENCES

Anthony, Kenneth R., *et. al.*, 1979, *Agricultural Change in Tropical Africa*, New York: Cornell University.
Boserup, Ester, 1970, *Woman's Role in Economic Development*, New York: St. Martins.
Bryson, Judy C., 1979, *Women and Economic Development in Cameroon*, Washington D.C.: United States Agency for International Development.
Champaud, Jacques, 1973, *Mom, Terrior Bassa*, Paris: ORSTOM.
Dorjahn, Vernon R., 1965, 'The Factor of Polygamy in African Demography' in Bascom, William R., and Herskovits, Melville J., (eds.) *Continuity and Change in African Cultures*, Chicago and London: University of Chicago.

Goody, Jack and Buckley, Joan, 1973, 'Inheritance and Women's Labour in Africa', *Africa*, Vol. 43.

Guyer, Jane, 1977, *The Women's Farming System, the Lekie Southern Cameroon*, Yaounde: ENSA.

Hay, Margaret, 1976, 'Luo Women and Economic Change During the Colonial Period', in Hafkin, Nancy J., and Bay, Edna G., (eds.) *Women in Africa*, Stanford, California: Stanford University.

Hellen, J. A., 1977, 'Legislation and Landscape: Some Aspects of Agrarian Reform and Agricultural Adjustment', in O'Keefe, Phil and Wiser, Ben, (eds.), *Landuse and Development*, London: International African Institute.

Kaberry, Phyllis M., 1952, *Women of the Grassfields: A Study of the Position of Women in Bamenda, British Cameroons*, London: HMSO.

Laburthe-Tolra, Philippe, 1975, *Minlaaba: Histoire et Société Traditionelle chez les Beti du Sud-Cameroun*, Thèse, University de Paris V.

Lewis, W. Arthur, 1954, 'Economic Development with Unlimited Supplies of Labor', *Manchester School*, Vol. 22.   .

Lewis, W. Arthur, 1972, 'Reflections on Unlimited Labor', *International Economics and Economic Development*, New York and London: Academic Press.

Lord Lugard, 1965, first published in 1922, *The Dual Mandate in Tropical Africa*, London: Frank Cass.

Martin, M. Kay, and Voorhies, Barbara, 1975, *Female of the Species*, New York and London: Columbia University.

Murdock, George P., 1967, 'Ethnographic Atlas: A Summary', *Ethnology*, Vol. 6, No. 4.

Ndongko, Theresa, 1976, 'Tradition and the Role of Women in Africa', *Presence Africaine*, No. 99/100.

Van Bath, B. H. S., 1963, *The Agrarian History of Western Europe A.D. 500–1850*, London.

Mobilising Village Women: Some Organisational and Management Considerations

by Nici Nelson *

If effective involvement of women in development projects is to take place, then concerted efforts must be made at both the policy level and at the level of organising and managing of projects to do this. This article explores some of the ways in which this could be done and some of the organisational difficulties which might arise. Using two extended case studies of Integrated Rural Development Programmes which had extensive commitments to the women residents of the region, this paper explores the ways in which women can be hired and trained to be field staff as well as the methods which could be used to utilise village women as so-called peasant staff on a local level. Ways in which the popular participation of local women can be ensured are discussed. In all these levels of participation, local mores on women's public role, as well as the social constraints which limit women's participation in the extra-domestic life of the community − things such as limited education, child care, and the female labour contribution to the domestic unit − must all be understood and incorporated into any strategies designed to invite and encourage the active participation of women.

I. INTRODUCTION

Since the early 1970s there has been much serious discussion on the role of women in national development. Ester Boserup's pioneer study, *Woman's Role in Economic Development* [*1970*], was one of the earliest. Since then increasing attention has been directed to different aspects of women and development in various parts of the Third World.[1] The message of these investigations is clear. Development processes have been run for and by men. Women have remained marginal to these processes and in some instances have actually been disadvantaged by them. This is a tragic waste of human resources. In the International Development Strategy for the UN Development Decade one of the goals and objectives of the decade is 'the full integration of women in the total development effort. Women's integration in development will benefit not only women but the whole society of men, women and children' [*Boserup, 1975:8*].

I feel that enough has been written to document the fact that women have been disadvantaged by development. It is now time to move ahead and to focus on the ways in which these disadvantages can be rectified. This is the purpose of this

---

* This paper was initially presented to a ODI Workshop on Administration and Organisation for Women In Agricultural Development under the title of 'Involving Women in Rural Development Process: Some Practical Considerations in the Areas of Policy, Organization and Management' on 23 March 1979.

paper. Integrating women into the total development effort first requires integrating them into all levels of policy-making (both as framers and as focuses of policy decisions). It means sensitising those in charge of the organisation and management of development projects to the need to hire women project staff, to involve village women in community participation exercises, as well as to consider the short- and long-term effects of any technical or economic inputs on women's lives. In this paper I present some initial thoughts on the subject, drawing on two detailed case studies: the IRAM report on the Animation for Women Project which was part of a larger integrated rural development scheme in Niger, Animation au Développement, begun in 1966 [*Barres, 1976*]; and the Abdullah and Zeidenstein assessment of the Pilot Project in Population Planning and Rural Women's Cooperatives which was part of the Bangladesh Integrated Rural Development Programme begun in 1974 [*1978*]. I hope to clarify some of the problems and difficulties facing projects which are designed for rural women. While I do not claim to offer any definitive solutions at this stage, tentative suggestions are made on how these problems might be overcome.

II. POLICY

Role of International Agencies

The first step in altering development strategy in regard to women must obviously be taken at the level of policy-making in the capital and in the International Agencies which fund and organise many projects in the Third World. Though things are far from ideal in the various unilateral and multilateral agencies, there are signs that at least they are receptive to the concept of involving women more meaningfully in development processes. The Percy Amendment in the United States recently made it mandatory for every USAID feasibility study of development projects to include a consideration of its effect on women, no matter how seemingly unrelated to traditional feminine spheres the project might be. Thus an assessment of a new hydroelectric project must contain such an assessment. Many country or regional missions of USAID have now hired an 'expert' on women to provide this input. The recent concern of UN Agencies with the Basic Needs Approach can also be seen as a step in the direction of recognising women's work burden and the need for technological innovation allowing women to contribute to the satisfaction of their families' basic needs in a less time-consuming and arduous manner [*Palmer, 1977*]. UNICEF is seriously considering expanding their mandate to include the funding of income-generating activities for Third World women. Though there is a long way to go, the signs are all favourable for continued improvement. International Agencies can play a strong advocacy role with governments and decision-makers, urging a more meaningful consideration of these issues.

Outside agencies can play a more active role than just advocacy for women *vis-à-vis* governments of Third World countries. These organisations can draft projects or set up requirements which make obligatory a consideration of women's position in the operations proposed for funding. These requirements will at least open the door to a dialogue at the policy proposal level. There is a danger that this dialogue will develop into a ritualised acknowledgement of the problem by government officials in order to obtain development funds. However, the attempt must be made. Once governments have made policy statements on an issue, indigenous local pressure groups might force those in authority to follow up rhetoric with action. To assist this process International Agencies can fund country-level research (preferably action-oriented) on rural women.

Research on Women

It is not the main purpose of this article to set out in detail the ways in which attitudes and approaches must be altered at a national policy-making level. However some tactics will be briefly outlined. There is initially a need for country-level research, data collection at a village level and analysis to establish the present socio-economic position of women, partly to explode current myths about their lack of importance to village economies and partly to examine in detail the factors that may facilitate or constrain the provision of wider opportunities for women. There is overall a dearth of information on women and the roles they play in society and economy, but relatively speaking there is a greater information gap on rural women. As an overview of the literature on women in South Asia revealed, only a tiny percentage of sources available on women dealt with rural women [*Nelson, 1979*]. This is more likely to be the case where the roles women play are privatised within the household, such as in Islamic countries. For example in Bangladesh many men are convinced that women do very little 'work', dismissing their contribution to household productivity as 'mere housework'. Such reports as Almagir's comprehensive profile of the lives and work of Bangladesh women [*1977*] go a long way to refute these beliefs. Each country must carry out its own research exercise within its different regions, since each will manifest its own particular combination of historical, cultural, social and economic factors. Experts who would never dream of applying generalised and stereotyped solutions to technical problems show a distressing tendency to think that issues involving women are simple and can be met with standardised panaceas everywhere. Women's Bureaux could be set up which would collate, collect and coordinate existing information as well as encourage, fund and partially direct future research. It is important that local scholars wherever possible take the lead in this research rather than depending on foreign experts.

Changes in Policy-Making Bodies

Knowledge is power, but only when it is used. This knowledge must be utilised to sensitise those in positions of power in government and civil service to the special problems of women in development. Ministers and civil servants must be convinced of the real national importance of actively integrating women in their development processes. To do this women's needs must be made explicit in reports and feasibility studies. Women must be included in high-level decision-making committees and more women recruited at all levels of national ministries, agencies and project staffs. It would be rash to assert that placing women in positions of power will automatically result in a better deal for rural women. Women appointed to such posts may be from the urban elite (notoriously ignorant about the conditions prevailing in rural areas for both men and women) and will have been trained in universities which reflect the 'male bias' of their societies. However, I feel that it is an important first step. The chances are greater that women will be more sensitive than men to the peculiar problems faced by other women. In addition, women in positions of public power can serve as important role models for male compatriots and other women demonstrating women's competence to deal with the larger world of politics and business. In the long term, such women may help to shift public opinion about women's proper roles.

III. ORGANISATION AND MANAGEMENT OF PROJECTS

For the sake of the discussion below we will assume an hypothetical case of an integrated rural development project which seeks to involve women within its jurisdiction more actively. This is partially because I feel that special isolated women's programmes have a smaller chance of success, and partially because the case studies I will refer to are examples of such a project. In this section I will discuss in turn three basic areas of the organisation and management of the aspects of the larger project concerning women. These will include staffing, selection and organisation of projects, and the popular participation of local women.

Government or Project Staff

The decision to expand the concerns of an integrated rural development programme means a serious rethinking in the area of staff. In most rural regions it is patently impossible for male project staff to deal effectively, if at all, with village women. 'In many countries, customs and cultural and religious constraints make it inappropriate for male agricultural extension agents to contact women directly' [*Dey, 1975:47*]. It has been assumed in the past that women will be influenced through their husbands; but this has often proved unsuccessful. A village woman's comment quoted in the IRAM report is revealing. 'It [fungicides and fertilisers] is for men ... everything brought to the village by a man is for men. If you women staff brought some in we could also have it'. [*Barres, 1976:34*].

(1) Recruitment. Once the decision is made to recruit women, the first obstacle will be a dearth of qualified women to fill the posts. In countries of South Asia or the Middle East, the level of female education lags lamentably far behind that of men. In other countries, such as those in South America, while women's literacy rates and University attendance compare favourably with those of men, women rarely qualify in the sciences, agriculture and other technical subjects. Thus when a project advertises for women to fill technical posts it may be difficult to find women with the same educational level as their male counterparts. The directors of the project may be forced to accept lower qualifications in order to obtain appropriate staff. This solution creates a further set of dilemmas. Will they obtain people with the proper skills and capabilities? Should they pay women of lower qualifications the same salaries for the same work as their more highly qualified male peers? To do so undermines the salary scales and can only serve to anger the men staff. Not to do so stamps the women staff as inferior. There are no easy answers to these questions. It may be assumed that with care capable women can be found, especially since women having suffered an educational disadvantage in

the past means that a woman's paper qualifications are not an accurate assessment of her innate qualities and ability to learn. Perhaps much could be done to train and further qualify women on the job, as was done in both the Bangladesh and Niger projects. Neither report made clear whether or not male project staff were similarly trained and whether or not the qualifications of the women staff were significantly lower than those of the men.

When women are recruited for the staff a number of criteria must be considered other than just academic training and personal commitment to the work. Often a choice will have to be made between more highly qualified young unmarried girls and older married women with a lower academic standard. Preference is often given to married women for two reasons. First it is assumed that due to local marriage patterns women will move out of the area to live with their husbands. Secondly, married women 'are preferred because their status enable[d] them more easily to have contact with village women' [Barres, 1976:79]. This is a personal characteristic which would be unimportant in the hiring of male staff. In Niger it was found that women Animation staff who were married worked better with village women and also fitted in with fewer complications with the male Animation teams. However, married women were less able to travel in the field or go for training outside of their home towns because of family responsibilities. This trade-off of stability/maturity and education/mobility is something which the project senior staff will have to settle; each particular socio-cultural region will impose its own individual demands on project staff.

(2) Staff Training. On the job training in the two case studies was extensive. In Bangladesh the women had pre-service training in class and on the job, regular in-service seminars, field trips, visits from headquarters staff, discussion groups and research assignments. Those who trained the staff attempted to counteract their naïve attitudes to rural women (whom many regarded as dirty, ignorant, and superstitious); taught methods of collecting basic information about rural women; stressed the importance of providing feedback from the village to those in charge of future planning for the project; gave technical training in whatever expertise the village staff needed to be taught (agricultural techniques, hygiene and family planning, literacy etc.); helped the new staff members to overcome their ignorance of, and embarrassment in, discussing sex and family planning; and transmitted general techniques of community organisation [Abdullah, 1978:166–183]. In Niger the new staff members received

> their training as part of their daily work, in the field and in conjunction with their activities, and periodically, by intensive and more theoretical sessions at the "department" and national levels. The fieldwork training included learning techniques of holding meetings, interviews, surveys, audio-visual techniques as well as methods of writing and using reports and thematic filing systems.' [Barres, 1976:79].

In neither report is the commensurate training given to men staff members mentioned. It would be ironic indeed if the special status of women staff members meant that they receive a more adequate on-the-job training.

Training may have to go beyond the transmission of technical information or methods of community organisation. It may be necessary to help women, even women of a high educational standard, to assert themselves in a group where men are present. Women may have to be encouraged at first to put their point of view across. Male staff members may have to learn to accept criticism and advice from female colleagues. All this involves a learning process running counter to deeply-held cultural beliefs about the proper behaviour of men and women.

(3) Conditions of work. When women have been recruited and are undergoing their training it will be important that as part of their training they share their experiences as pioneers. In order to lessen the shock of criticism and hostile attitudes of family, villagers and male staff members, women could hold discussions to air their feelings and their common experiences. I once met the first and only local woman field officer in the Pakistan office of a UN agency. She spoke movingly of the loneliness and isolation of being the only female in her office. It would also be helpful to hire more than one woman for any particular level of the hierarchy to prevent this isolated, threatening situation. Male staff members may experience strain working alongside a woman, much less under a woman superior. This conflict is not unique to the Third World, but it is bound to be exacerbated by any lack of familiarity with the situation of unrelated people of both genders working together on an equal basis. Would it also be useful to include male staff members in some of the discussions on the awkwardness of adjusting to new working conditions? While I am not suggesting anything as self-consciously therapeutic as work encounter groups, it is true that the problems of accommodating to new relationships between the genders in a work environment lie on both sides.

Practical suggestions can be made to minimize the initial shock of integrating women into a male project staff. Firstly women could be formed into autonomous sub-sections within the larger organisation thus keeping to a minimum any contact between men and women in the carrying out of their duties. Secondly, if this is not done women can be recruited in groups, as was suggested above. In the beginning it might be wiser to hire older married women who will be subject to less teasing and command more respect from their male compatriots. The aforementioned Pakistani field officer was young, attractive and unmarried; all of which no doubt contributed to the unmerciful ragging and hostility she met with. But the most important variable is that of numbers, I am sure. Women in pairs or groups can give each other the support and companionship important to neutralise possible negative reactions from colleagues and villagers. In Bangladesh it was found that having women extension staff move from village to village in pairs was enough to defuse village leaders' objections to these 'loose moraled' women allowed to wander about the countryside unattended.

Women extension workers may have greater difficulty travelling in the countryside than their male equivalents. Special recognition of this fact may have to be made in the form of larger travel allowances. Women in Bangladesh found it impossible (due to custom) to walk between villages. They were not allowed to ride bicycles or motor scooters and were forced to take taxis. This is culturally variable and in some regions moving the women in pairs may be a sufficient protection of their respectability. In other areas even this precaution may be unnecessary.

Finally care must be taken within the management of the project to give responsibility equally to men and women staff, while possibilities for personal initative by women in the organisation should not be discouraged. Proper rewards for initiative and hard work must be given in wage scales and promotion. To create a second class female staff will only undermine staff morale and serve to underline the feeling that those parts of the project related to women are second best.

Selecting and Structuring Specific Projects for Women

In many instances when steps are taken to include a women's programme in an on-going project, organisers may assume that a viable programme for rural women has already evolved and simply has to be implemented. In both the Bangladesh and Niger projects this was not the case and the women's component of the larger project had to be created with care, village level research and consultation with village women.

(1) Data Gathering as a First Step. The Bangladesh women's Pilot Project had to collect information about rural women as well as to evaluate new approaches to development. They had to face the question of whether or not rural staff could be recruited and who they would be, how they could be trained and how well they should be supervised. Careful consideration and consultation were held to help village women evolve their own economic programmes. Methods were sought to involve increasing numbers of women and various issues were explored relating to training rural women [*Abdullah, 1978:147–51*]. The exact methods employed in the gathering of data and the framing of future activities were not described in the document. In the training stage for the women staff they spent long periods in the village. This served the double purpose of familiarising the staff with village life as well as providing feed-back to Headquarters about the response of local women to the guidelines. It was stressed that rural women should determine the future of the project [*ibid:174–9*].

Similarly the methods of the Animation project in Niger began with a global survey done by the Animation staff. The women lived for weeks at a time in villages, sharing the living conditions of the villagers. The data that they collected were fed back to the villagers at meetings in order to stimulate discussion and some qualitative assessment was reached of the quantitative data collected in the survey. When certain priority problems were isolated, specific surveys were instituted and further discussions held at a village level. Women were urged to clarify for themselves those problems which they could solve themselves and those needing outside assistance [*Barres, 1976:68–70*].

It is important that this period of data gathering and consultation with village women and men take place. It cannot be assumed that approaches and problems as perceived by men will be adequate or meaningful for village women. Male bias in official expertise must be eliminated since if women are to be mobilised, or are to mobilise themselves, in order to perform certain activities, they must be those which *they* see as of high priority, not the ones valued by village men or project staff. At this stage compromise may have to be sought between what women value most highly and what men will initially permit. In Niger the first projects implemented were childcare and health projects because they were both important to women and acceptable to men. Once the positive effects of such programmes are felt it may be possible to proceed gradually to other more controversial areas of action.

Finally it is important that female staff have experience and exposure to village conditions. In many countries educated women (usually coming from the upper strata of society) may come from towns and be lamentably ignorant of the realities of village life. The same is of course true of educated men, but often women have been even more sheltered from harshness and poverty than men and so will profit from such an introduction to village women's lives.

(2) *Structuring of Women's Projects.* There is no single structure ideal for development projects for women. The two case studies demonstrate entirely different approaches to the problem. The Bangladesh project utilises women's village cooperatives to organise economic and family planning activities. Staff members call a village meeting to talk to men and to convince them to allow their women to participate in the project. When the women have gathered, the staff question them about the type of programme they wish. Frequently the initial reaction is to suggest home development activities, such things as embroidery or cooking, which are the only type of 'women's programmes' with which the villagers are familiar. The staff are at pains to point out the inapplicability of approaches such as these. The staff urge the women to form cooperatives in order to achieve through group strength solutions to problems which they see as important, and to apply to government agencies for necessary services. Women are asked to decide what to do by way of an economic activity based on what they already know [*Abdullah, 1978:185–202*]. Once the decision has been taken to form a cooperative, five women are selected as representatives to make a weekly trip to the district headquarters for training. These leaders communicate relevant information, supplies, and services to the cooperative members when they return to the village.

Cooperative members have to buy a share before joining the organisation in order to give each member a sense of economic commitment to the cooperative. Regular weekly meetings are mandatory to encourage group decision-making and to permit the transmission of information or materials from extension workers and cooperative leaders. Cooperatives can apply for loans on the basis of a production plan developed by members with the help of cooperative leaders and staff. The loans are actually given to individual project members for their own activities, but the repayment of the loan is a group responsibility. All of it must be repaid by the repayment date before any other loans can be made. While the production plan is being worked out, the staff give classes on loan procedures, production plans and uses of loans which are both profitable and productive (for instance, members are urged not to use loans to fund hoarding activities). How the loan is allocated amongst the members is left to the individual cooperative to decide [*ibid:221–33*].

In contrast the Animation project in Niger opted for a more *ad hoc* project approach attacking different issues often in collaboration with other ministries. It was not clear whether these projects included all or only selected villages in an area. The procedure followed by the Animation de Développement project was to select and train local peasant animators in order to encourage voluntary participation of peasants in development. This method 'of promoting peasant participation provides results more slowly at the outset but gives positive results in the long run' [*Barres, 1976:71*]. It hopefully introduces a self-sustaining process which transforms the type of work done by government or project staff.

The government staff participate at the level of training the animators, supporting village projects, and making plans at the level of groups of villages.

There is nothing in the above which could not apply equally to organisations structured for men. Several generalisations can be made which are specific to projects organised for women. First, in recognition of local social realities the acceptance of the men of the villages must be obtained before any work can be begun. Men have to be convinced that letting women participate in development activities outside of the home has more advantages than disadvantages. In certain cultures men may need more persuasion than in others.

Secondly, it cannot be assumed that the structures which are effective in mobilising village men will automatically be effective for the women. In Bangladesh the IRD Programme has operated on the basis of all-village cooperatives for men. There is some reason to believe that the law which allows only one cooperative per village may be a barrier to a more effective type of organisational structure for women. The para (or cluster of related households) may initially be a more realistic unit for female cooperative membership. It seems that some women may be barred from membership in the cooperative because they are not allowed to travel freely outside of their own para. Perhaps it would be possible to set up branches of the village cooperative in each para? Imagination and flexibility are important when structuring development programmes in general, and for women's programmes in particular.

(3) Choosing Peasant Staff. Many of the difficulties attached to training government or project staff mentioned above apply to the training of village or peasant staff. There are differences related to the lower economic background, status, and education levels of the village staff women. At the village level it may be difficult to obtain young women, married or not, for such posts. Local tradition may decree that such unmarried girls be sequestered in their father's household, while married women with small children may be prevented from participating by pressures of childcare or duties to older female relatives. These are not insurmountable obstacles as can be seen in Operation Midwife in Niger where the village women themselves decided that the midwives to be sent for training had to be young and strong enough to learn new techniques [*Barres, 1976:72*]. Again the organisers may be faced with a choice of either age and experience or youth and higher educational standards. In contrast to the case with the government staff, it is likely that older women will be more mobile than unmarried girls on the village level because social convention is a stronger force amongst the rural peasantry than it is among the educated elite. This again will vary from place to place.

The selection of peasant staff is bound to reflect the hierarchical nature of the village rather than the individuals' capacity to fulfil a function. In Bangladesh this was recognised but little seemed to be done to combat it. It was hoped that women of higher status in the village would provide role models for change to poorer, lower status women, while recognising the danger that they might co-opt the resources of the cooperative for themselves. The Animation project in Niger tried to counter this elitism by increasing the number of women animators in each village while providing skills training necessary for successful performance of short-term tasks. Women of no recognisable status were able to assert themselves by using their abilities. This is a problem that will be faced by all organisations which attempt to mobilise grass roots popular participation. However poor rural women may find it more difficult than poor rural men to assume group leadership and initiative in an organisation which includes women of a higher status. Higher status rural women, though they may be subordinate to the men of their family and class, may also have had experience in directing the labour of other men and women. This is an advantage in developing the habit and ideology of leadership. Admittedly this point is speculative, but it is one which deserves consideration.

(4) Training of Peasant Staff. When considering the training of peasant staff, questions of travel and distance from the village to training centres are important. Women, by the nature of their domestic responsibilities as well as the constraints placed on them by culture, will usually be unable to stay away from home for extended periods of training. For this reason it would be useful if training centres were small and decentralised, designed to serve adjacent villages as was done by the Niger Animation Project.

Where this is not possible because an existing infrastructure must be used, as in Bangladesh, care must be taken to ensure that proper travel arrangements and accommodation are provided. Travel allowances may have to be higher and accommodation will have to be segregated and unquestionably 'respectable' to avoid censure by village leaders. It may even be reasonable to provide child care facilities at such training centres so that poor women without relatives able to care for small children would be able to travel with their babies.

Training of women peasant staff will be made more difficult by the relatively greater illiteracy and lack of specific skills of these women compared to rural men. Training given to women in such fields as book-keeping, loan procedures, record-keeping, or indeed any mechanical skills may have to be more intensive than that given to men. Women in many areas simply lack experience with forms, government bureaucracies and regulations.

Popular Participation of Village Women

When the staff of a development project wish to gather village women in groups or to approach them singly for whatever purpose, certain considerations must be kept in mind.

(1) Convening Women in Public Meetings. Local custom may make it awkward for women to meet in public places. Where this is the case, then government staff must try to circumvent these restrictions. Perhaps holding a series of smaller meetings in the homes of more prestigious families will be necessary at first. (This also has its dangers, making it appear as if the development activity will be run by the higher status families.) Perhaps the staff could persuade the village leaders to set aside a certain place, such as the school-room after hours, for the use of the women. Eventually, perhaps, a women's centre could be built which would incorporate clinic, health and family planning centre, and rooms for meetings, classes and economic activities.

(2) Timing of Activities. The timing of contact activities for development programmes is of prime importance in ensuring large-scale participation of village women. It must be remembered that rural women often have less free time than their menfolk, especially where they are actively involved in productive activities along with their domestic responsibilities. Public meetings, training sessions and

trips for peasant staff must be scheduled at times convenient for local women, especially the poorest and often most overworked women, rather than for that of the government staff. For example, it may be necessary to suspend training etc. in the harvest season or other periods of women's peak labour contribution.

(3) *Child Care Facilities.* If programmes are set up which include training programmes or economic activities which will take place outside of the home, there must be provision for child care made at the same time. This can be done in a variety of ways. The crèche could be run communally by the women themselves, or child-minders could be paid to run the crèche on a full or part time basis. If this is not the case, mothers with small children may be unable to attend or young daughters will be forced to care for their younger siblings to the detriment of their schooling.

(4) *Utilising Traditional Women's Associations or Groups.* Where women already have traditional organisations, in some cases it might be sensible to utilise these (at least in the beginning) as a means of approaching women to instigate a dialogue between local women and between them and the project staff on the future structuring of development activities. Women's age group associations, saving societies, or even networks of kin and friends could provide these initial contact points. Whether or not they will provide the structure for future organisation will depend on each particular context. For instance, how homogeneous are these local groups? How much do they reflect local hierarchies? Do they have the organisational potential to expand to include the bureaucratic and training inputs of a development project? Since women in many rural areas (and I reiterate that this is highly variable) are often difficult for outsiders to approach, the initial use of traditional organisations may be a way which is less threatening, both for village women and their men.

IV. CONCLUSION

Some of the considerations special to programmes which aim to involve women in development processes have been set out. First, the necessity of effecting changes at a national policy level was discussed and it was suggested that International Agencies take a strong role in advocacy in this area while at the same time providing funds for projects which include a meaningful consideration of women's lives and socio-economic roles. The importance of country-level research on women, perhaps organised by a Women's Bureau, was stressed as well as co-opting women to decision-making bodies at a national and regional level or to ministries and civil service at all levels.

I then addressed myself to the special problems which might be encountered in the organisation and management of projects which are directed wholly or in part towards village women. It must be stressed that one should not generalise.

Two case studies, one from Niger and one from Bangladesh, were used to illustrate my arguments. The three major headings under which I discussed organisational and management issues were those of government staff, the selection and organisation of specific development activities and popular participation of local women.

The overriding importance of recruiting women staff and the possible difficulties of locating qualified individuals were emphasised. Hiring of female extension staff entails consideration of qualities normally unimportant in staff recruitment – qualities such as marital status, age and mobility. Some of the ways in which staff training and conditions of work would have to be adjusted were discussed.

In selecting specific development projects for women, the need for local consultation with women and men is of prime importance. Though no magic formula exists for deciding on a structure for projects for rural women, several factors must be kept in mind whatever structure is decided upon. Village men must be first convinced of its importance. It must respect local ideals of women's proper role in society. This means that the solutions applied locally to male development projects cannot be automatically assumed to be useful for organising women. Choosing and training of peasant staff presents its own specific aspects of selection criteria, travel and accommodation.

Mobilising village women may be easy or difficult depending on local tradition regarding women in the public arena. The constraints on convening women for public meetings, the importance of scheduling development activities, the need for child care facilities and the possibility of utilising already existing women's groups all must be considered.

NOTE

1. For a representative sample, see Boserup, [1975]; Buvenic, [1976]; Nelson, [1979]; Palmer, [1977]; *Signs* special issue on women and national development, [1977]; Shaukat, [1975]; Tinker, [1976].

REFERENCES

Abdullah and Zeidenstein, 1978, *Village Women of Bangladesh: Prospects for Change*, Geneva: ILO.
Alamagir, Susan, 1977, *Profile of Bangladesh Women: Selected Aspects of Women's Roles and Status in Bangladesh*, Dacca: USAID.
Barres, V., 1976, *The Participation of Rural Women in Development: A Project of Rural Women's Animation in Niger 1966–75*, Paris: IRAM.
Boserup, Ester, 1970, *Woman's Role in Economic Development*, London: George Allen and Unwin.
—, 1975, *Integration of Women in Development: Why, When, How?* UN Development Programme.
Buvenic, Mayra, 1976, *Women in Development: An Annotated Bibliography*, Overseas Development Council.
Dey, J. M., 1975, *The Role of Women in Rural Development in Third World Countries: Some Aspects of Relevance to Policy Makers*, MA Thesis, University of Reading.
Nelson, Nici, 1979, *Why Has Development Neglected Rural Women? A Review of the South Asian Literature*, Oxford: Pergamon.
Palmer, Ingrid, 1975, 'Women in Rural Development', Unpublished paper.
—, 1977, 'Rural Women and the Basic Needs Approach to Development', *International Labour Review*, Vol. 115.
Stimpson, C. (ed.), 1977, *Signs: Journal of Women in Culture and Society*, Special Issue on Women and National Development, Vol. 3, No. 1.
Shaukat, Ali Parveen, 1975, *The Women in the Third World: A Comprehensive Bibliography with an Introductory Essay*, Lahore: Progressive Publishers.
Tinker, Irene (ed.), 1976, *Women and World Development*, Washington, D.C: Overseas Development Council.

An Analysis of the Impact of Labour Migration on the Lives of Women in Lesotho

by Elizabeth Gordon *

The women of Lesotho live their lives in reaction to the overwhelming outmigration of their men to work in South Africa. At any time, 40 to 60 per cent of married women are living as wives of absent men. A number of viewpoints on these women's lives in the light of this are apparent; in particular, one describing their position as extremely difficult, and another, by contrast, postulating supports that would mitigate this difficulty. The present study represents the first empirical investigation of the wives' lives in their husbands' absence. Five hundred and twenty-four wives of absent migrants were studied throughout Lesotho. Data were obtained as to the women's characteristics, attitudes, and, through the development of a strain score, those in the greatest difficulty. The findings suggested a process by which wives of migrants find themselves in increasing difficulty and supported the view of the wives' position as extremely difficult. It did not support those positing mitigating circumstances. Speculation as to conditions extant in Lesotho which contribute to this difficulty was presented and accordingly, discretion urged in applying conclusions to other settings.

THE IMPACT OF LABOUR MIGRATION ON FAMILY LIFE

The specific conditions of labour migration in Lesotho, and its extent, ensure its profound impact on marital life. The conditions are determined by South African law. When the men cross the border to work in South Africa, they leave their families behind in the villages and towns of Lesotho, as women and children are prohibited from living with a migrant worker. South African law also dictates that the migrant worker cannot remain continually in South Africa for more than two years: he must return to Lesotho, for at least a period of leave, when two years have elapsed.

These conditions make for a migration pattern known as oscillating [*Nattrass, 1975:2*]. The familiar pattern is for the migrant to leave his family in the home village, work in South Africa for a period of time, return to his family for as long as he feels is economically feasible, and once again, to cross the border to work.

It is clear that under these conditions a range of interaction types exists between a man and his family during his work contract. The nature of the interactions is

---

* The study on which this paper is based has been undertaken in the framework of the Southern African research programme on international migration and employment of the ILO's World Employment Programme. The views in this paper are not necessarily those of the International Labour Office.

determined by the migrant's circumstances and motivations. Some men remain in close contact with their family. They seek a location for work in South Africa whose proximity to Lesotho allows for close contact, with frequent week-end visits home. At the other end of the spectrum, there are men who find in the migrant labour system a way to abandon their families with comparative ease. They vanish into the complexities of life in South Africa and are not seen again by their families for many years, if ever. Mandatory leaves in Lesotho are spent in the capital city, with no visit to the home village being made before the return to work in South Africa. In between these extremes are men who maintain some degree of contact with their families, perhaps coming home yearly at Christmas, or every two-years when work contracts end.

The extent of labour migration in Lesotho is determined by the paucity of wage-earning opportunities within the country, and by the fact that working in South Africa, especially in the mines, has become a tradition for its men. Its extent can be measured both in terms of the number of men involved in the system, and the number of years they are away during their working lives.

It has been estimated that approximately half the adult male labour force of Lesotho is away working in South Africa at any time, with a much higher percentage who work there at some point in their lives [Cobb, 1976:2]. To further understand what the large number of absent males means for family life, an estimate can be made of the number of married women living as wives of absent migrants at any one time. Determining the number of migrants working out of the country, and the proportion of these who are married, enables this to be approximated.

The exact figures for men working outside Lesotho are difficult to obtain, except for mine workers, on whom statistics are kept by the recruitment offices and the Department of Labour. Figures for 1976 indicate an average of 121,161 Basotho working in the mines of South Africa at any point in time [Department of Labour, Maseru, Lesotho]. Applying a marriage rate of 70 per cent to this figure,[1] leads to the conclusion that the miners leave behind close to 85,000 wives living in Lesotho. If the wives of the 30,000 to 80,000 men working as migrants in agriculture, construction and other industries are added, the number left behind reaches more than 100,000 and may approach 150,000. The 1976 Census indicates that 234,159 married women reside in Lesotho. Thus, it appears that 40 to 60 per cent of married women in the country live as wives of absent migrants at any one time [Bureau of Statistics, Maseru, Lesotho].

Not only are the effects of migration extensive in terms of the number of wives affected, but also, the long periods which the average migrant works away from home must have serious repercussions on their families' lives. McDowall, studying the records of a mining company that is the largest employer of Basotho men, found that the average miner spends 35 per cent of his working life in the mines, a total of approximately 15 years away from home, and that he tends to migrate when in his twenties, thirties and forties [McDowall, 1974]. Van der Wiel, in a field survey, found twenty to be the average age at which migrants first go to work with approximately a third retiring before 40 years old, and about two-thirds by the age of 50. He estimated the number of years a migrant worker spends abroad to be 16 for those coming from the lowlands and 13 for those from the mountain zone [Van der Wiel, 1977:51]. The migrant worker, therefore, appears to be largely absent during the critical years of his marriage and much of the childhood years of his children. For wives in Lesotho, marital life largely follows the cyclical career of migrant husbands; couples live apart for much of their married lives, coming together on the husbands' leaves and visits home, the periods between contracts if the husbands remain at home, and, perhaps eventually, upon the man's retirement.[2]

Controversies Relating to the Women's Lives in Their Husbands' Absence

Although it is clear that labour migration has a great impact on the lives of the women left behind, the specific nature of that impact has not been determined. There appears to be a number of schools of thought regarding women in such positions, and in Lesotho in particular. One stresses the dire effects of labour migration on family life. Two others view the situation as not so critical, asserting that mitigating circumstances exist of which the casual observer may not be aware. Each of these second two viewpoints assumes a different set of supports for the wife which lessens her apparent difficulty. These three views will be discussed below.

Observers pointing to the disastrous effects of labour migration on family life in Lesotho, describe the wife's position as one of loneliness, helplessness and poverty.[3] Her children are seen as being raised solely by her own efforts, and the lack of a father's presence as boding ill for their development. The migrant's wife is pictured as remaining under her husband's ultimate power and control: although she is left to shoulder an unbearable burden of responsibility for family affairs, and property − particularly fields and livestock − she has little decision-making power in regards to these. She is considered to 'usually lack the innovational decision-making ability whenever the head of the household is male and that male is absent ...' [Williams, 1971:161]. The husband insists on retaining the right to make decisions, while the wife implements them. It has been asserted that, 'The absent men have such authority that forward looking well-educated wives are afraid to innovate for fear their husbands will disapprove.' [Gay, no date:9]. The wife knows that should she be accused of mismanagement of family resources upon her husband's return home, she will have to face his considerable wrath.

One of the more positive viewpoints emphasises that labour migration has become a fact of life in Lesotho. It is seen as having been part of the culture for so long, and being so widespread, that it has become the norm to which family life has adjusted. Women grow up expecting to live in a separated family situation from the moment they begin to think of marriage; they plan for it and function comfortably in their husbands' absence. As the norm is separated families with few children having resident fathers for the course of their childhood, effects upon children are felt to be minimal. An additional assumption brought to bear is that the extended family largely fulfils the functions of the absent husband and father. Kinsmen are seen as taking over his responsibilities with regard to family and property, especially fields and livestock, making the effects of his absence less than profound. It has been asserted, for example, in regard to West Africa, that when men are away 'the extended family of the migrants can step up their efforts and cooperative work groups can fill in such manpower gaps as arise.' [Berg,

1965:167]. A description of the wives of migrants as being in substantial difficulty would presumably be felt, from this standpoint, as being an initial, cursory impression which does not take the specific realities of Basotho life into consideration, and which could be criticised as ethnocentrically and inappropriately applying Western conceptions of the nuclear family to an African situation.

Another viewpoint that minimizes the damaging social effects of labour migration, points to its emancipating function for the wives. The ties of the extended family are seen as having been loosened, partially due to labour migration itself which absents many men from the family and kin group and leaves few men available to take over the responsibilities of those away. Left without recourse to assistance from their husbands, or substantial aid from kinsmen, the wives are viewed as learning to function independently. It has been asserted that in Southern Africa, 'The very fact that most women are for varying periods left alone while their husbands work elsewhere means that they have to assume a range of responsibilities that formerly rested on men, or at least the extended family which is also tending to grow smaller and diminish in importance.' [*Moody, 1976:27*]. Women have, accordingly, been described as having largely taken over the responsibility for agriculture in Southern Africa [*ibid*]. In terms of sub-Saharan Africa, the effects of labour migration have been similarly described:

> Given the periodic absence of the husband and father, as well as of other male kinsmen, a new independence is given to the domestic unit of woman and her children. Whereas formerly the woman was a deputy for the husband ... frequently enough today the women is left in full charge not only of her children but also of the property belonging to the absent male. She makes the day-to-day decisions and may also make long-term decisions which the man must accept when he returns home. [*Colson, 1970:155*].

It is accordingly concluded that labour migration 'has given women in many instances the opportunity to develop as undisputed heads of their domestic units.' [*Ibid*]. Women are seen as enjoying this independent role, welcoming the freedom of action their husbands' absence allows. A description of labour migration as having dire effects on the family would according to this viewpoint, fail to consider the new role for women that has developed, and their resultant satisfaction with the situation.

In the absence of empirical work on migrants' families in Lesotho, it had been impossible to resolve these varying viewpoints as to the position of the wives in the men's absence. Is the view that these women are in substantial difficulty, in actuality the viewpoint of the naïve observer, who fails to take more subtle developments into consideration? Do there exist supports, either in the form of assistance from kinsmen or from within a new independent role for women, that enable their lives to be free of undue difficulty? These questions, central to an understanding of the wives' position, remained unanswered.

THE STUDY

The present study was developed against this background; the knowledge that labour migration had a clearly-existing impact on family life in Lesotho, but that the specific nature of that impact was uncertain. A better understanding of the wives' lives in their husbands' absence was felt to be necessary; one not based on speculation or theory as to what their situation should be, but rather, an empirical study of the wives themselves, to discern how they lived. Because there was no background of established facts on which to build, no previous studies focusing on the women of Lesotho, this research was seen, by necessity, to be exploratory in nature. As a pilot study, it did not set out to prove or disprove a particular theory, but rather to be a first attempt to gain some idea of the quality of the women's lives. It was felt, however, that a number of issues explored in the study would directly pertain to the different viewpoints discussed above and that a better general understanding of the situation would shed some light on them.

The study, then, focused on the wives themselves − a representative sample large enough to support conclusions − and asked them to describe their situation as they perceived it. It explored their characteristics, attitudes and problems. It attempted to identify those wives having the greatest difficulty in their husbands' absence, and the factors that related to this difficulty. In this way, a picture of the women's lives in their husbands' absence was gradually developed.

Research Methodology

The research involved a large-scale field survey of wives of migrant workers living in Lesotho.[4] Data was collected at 14 randomly-selected sites throughout the country, using a structured questionnaire administered in personal, individual interviews. The sample sites were heterogeneous as to size, and varied as to the ecological zone of the country and accessibility to the capital.

The questionnaire was written and administered in Sesotho, the native tongue. It contained questions as to the wives' demographic characteristics, their husbands' characteristics, and their attitudes towards a number of aspects of their situation. These included the raising of children in the husbands' absence, responsibility for fields and livestock, anxiety about providing for the family, and their greatest problems in their husbands' absence. Both open-ended and closed questions were included, where each seemed appropriate. Interviewers were third and fourth year students from the Social Science Faculty of the National University. They were native Sesotho speakers with a good command of English, who underwent extensive interviewer training.

At each location, every household was contacted, and all wives of migrant workers absent in South Africa were interviewed. Only women whose husbands were working in South Africa at the time of interview were included. Every effort was made to reach all 'eligible' wives. Because the field procedure involved the research teams camping at a site for an extensive period, callbacks were usually successful. For each site, half the completed questionnaires were randomly selected to be analysed.[5] Five hundred and twenty-four interviews with wives of migrant workers thus formed the study sample.

The questionnaires were edited and coded by a team of research assistants under the constant supervision of the senior researcher. All coders were native Sesotho speakers so that questionnaires could be read in their original form. Coding accuracy was checked by the senior researcher. The data were then entered on computer cards and a computer programme for identifying coding errors was run. All such errors were rectified before the data analysis.

Data Analysis

The data analysis had four main objectives. First, the study aimed at describing the wives, developing a picture of who they are, the men they are married to and the households they live in. The second goal involved a delineation of their feelings and attitudes towards the situation in which they find themselves, and the association of a number of these with relevant independent variables. The third concern was to determine those areas in which the wives experience the greatest problems in their husbands' absence.

The final goal of the analysis, perhaps the most ambitious, was to identify those wives who appear to be in the worst circumstances; those having the greatest difficulty functioning in their husbands' absence, and experiencing the greatest degree of dissatisfaction. To this end, ten of the 22 attitude questions were developed as items clearly indicating difficulty or dissatisfaction. These questions queried such areas as whether the wife worried about the welfare of her family, felt she had too many responsibilities, was satisfied with her husband's role in various family activities, and whether she would be happier if he were home more. Each question was answered with 'yes' or 'no' and was worded so that for some questions greater difficulty or strain was indicated by a positive answer, and for others, by a negative one. All items used to indicate strain were totally unambiguous as to the direction of response that indicated greater difficulty or dissatisfaction. These questions were dispersed among the other attitude questions.

A strain score was calculated for each wife, based on her answers to these ten attitudinal questions. The number of questions she answered in the direction indicating strain ('yes' or 'no', as the case may be) was divided by the total number for which she gave a response. Unanswered questions, those irrelevant to a particular wife, or those for whom an answer of 'don't know' was given, were excluded from consideration. The resultant fraction was changed to a decimal. The strain scores thus ranged from 0, lowest possible strain, to 100, highest possible strain. The association of strain score with other research variables could then be examined, enabling a profile of the wives experiencing the greatest difficulty to be established. The circumstances associated with a high degree of subjective strain could thus be indicated.

Directed towards these goals, the computer analysis began with a frequency listing of all variables describing the wives, the migrant husbands and the households. Frequency listing of the wives' greatest problems and their answers to the attitude questions were effected in the same initial computer run. The strain score of each wife was tabulated and a frequency distribution of these obtained. Cross-tabulations were carried out between relevant variables, and especially, between the strain score and other variables. The significance of each cross-tabulation was tested using chi-square analysis, with level of acceptance at $p = .05$.

Results

Demographic Characteristics.[6] The wives were found to be a relatively young group: their mean age was 29, with 65 per cent of the sample 30 years old or younger, and only 5 per cent over 45 years old. Seventy-eight per cent were wives of the head of the households in which they were living, 19 per cent being related as daughters-in-law. Fifteen per cent had no children. For those women who did have children, the majority (67 per cent) had three or less, 34 per cent had four or more. The mean number of children for the entire sample, including those with no children was 2.5. For those women who had at least one child, the average was 2.9. Forty per cent of the wives were married after 1970, and 62 per cent after 1965. Only 10 per cent were married before 1956.

Their husbands were also a young group, only slightly older than their wives. Sixty-three per cent were 35 years old or younger, with 40 per cent aged 30 or below. Only 6 per cent were over 45. Sixty-two per cent of the husbands had some schooling; 11 per cent having gone up to standard 3, 30 per cent having passed standard 4 to standard 6, and 18 per cent having gone higher than standard 6. The great majority of the men (86 per cent), were miners. Seven per cent worked in construction and 5 per cent in factories. Those who were miners tended to work in gold mines, with 76 per cent so employed. An additional 10 per cent worked in coal mines, and 6 per cent in platinum mines. For those for whom the year they first worked as a migrant was known, 48 per cent began working as migrants after 1965, and 68 per cent after 1960. Nineteen per cent had their first migrant employment in 1955, or prior to that. For those for whom the number of years worked in South Africa could be calculated, 60 per cent had spent a total of one to ten years away, 78 per cent had spent one to 15 years away, and 9 per cent had worked over twenty years as migrants.

Of the households in which the wives lived, 53 per cent included one migrant member, 33 per cent had two, and 15 per cent, three or more. Most households included from four to seven people. Sixty per cent of the households were located in the lowlands of the country, 26 per cent in the foothills and 14 per cent in the mountains. A male was head in 92 per cent of the households, and a female in eight per cent. A migrant worker was household head in 82 per cent of the sample – a non-migrant in 18 per cent. Household income was considered as inadequate by 66 per cent of the households, 34 per cent considering its income adequate for living expenses. For 90 per cent, household income was received only from migrants. Nine per cent had an additional income source.

Greatest Problems Experienced in Husbands' Absence. Wives were asked their greatest problem in their husbands' absence, and their second greatest problem. In terms of greatest problem, 30 per cent of the wives felt they had no problem, 37 per cent cited a problem related to fields and livestock, and those remaining mentioned problems in other areas. The percentage of wives responding that they had no greatest problem decreased steadily as age increased, the youngest group most likely (51 per cent), to give this response. The proportion of wives citing a greatest problem related to agriculture, increased as age increased. By age group 26–30, 45 per cent of the wives mentioned a problem in this area. This increased to 49 per cent for the 31–40 year olds, and to 50 per cent for those wives over 40 years of age. Noticeable among greatest problems mentioned in other areas were those related to illness and medical care, (9 per cent) and those related to lack of food (6 per cent). Half of the wives did not feel they had a second problem. Of those who did cite a problem about a quarter mentioned one that was agriculture-related and the same proportion, one that was illness-related.

Thus, the problems that the wives report themselves as experiencing in their husbands' absence are largely those that arise in connection with management of fields and livestock. Of those wives citing a problem, over half (55 per cent) mentioned one in this area as their greatest problem, and over a quarter, 28 per cent, as their second greatest problem. Difficulties encountered in connection with health and obtaining medical care appear to be a second area of concern for the wives, especially when these involve children.

Wives' Attitudes towards Family Life in their Husbands' Absence

The wives' answers to the 22 attitude questions[7] were as follows:

An overwhelming majority (77 per cent[8] or more) feel that:
1. It is important for a father to help bring up his children.
2. If their husband were offered a job in Lesotho with the same pay he is now getting as a migrant, they would like him to accept it.
3. Their husband carries out all his responsibilities towards his children.
4. Even when their husband is away he still continues to make important decisions concerning the family.
5. They worry about the general welfare of their family.

An extremely large majority (74–75 per cent) feel that:
1. They worry about their children's future.
2. They worry about being able to raise their children well.
3. They would lead a much happier life if their husband could be home much more often than is the case now.
4. The problems they meet with regard to their children would be reduced if their husband could be home all the time.
5. When their husbands are away, the family fields and livestock are their responsibility.

A large majority (71–72 per cent) feel that:
1. They worry about being able to feed themselves and their children.
2. They don't agree that they enjoy the independence they get when their husband is away.
3. They are satisfied with the part their husband plays in taking care of the family fields and livestock.
4. Their children miss their father when he is away.
5. They worry about being able to buy clothes for themselves and their children.

A sizeable majority (60–66 per cent) feel that:
1. When their husbands are away, they are the one making important decisions concerning the family.
2. When their husband is away, they have too many family responsibilities.
3. They don't agree that they would have liked it to be possible to go and live with their husbands at his place of work.

A majority (52–59 per cent) feel that:
1. They are satisfied with the amount of money their husband sends home.
2. They don't agree that as long as there are male adults – related to the family – to help raise the children, it does not matter whether their children's father is present or not.
3. They worry about paying for their children's school fees.
4. Their husband visits home often enough from his place of work.

Strain Score

The distribution of strain scores was found to be normal at $p = .05$, using the Kolmogorov-Smirnov test. For use in cross-tabulations, the sample was divided into three strain score groups. The low stress group, with scores ranging from 0 to 40, was 28 per cent of the sample. The medium strain score group, with scores from 41 to 60, was 34 per cent of the sample. The high strain group, with scores over 60, was 38 per cent of the total.

The Low Strain Score Group. The wives most likely to have low stress scores had a consistent group of characteristics. They were the youngest wives, married most recently, with either no children or one child. Their husbands were in the youngest age group, had started working as migrants most recently, and had worked the fewest years as migrants. These women were either related to the head of the household as daughter-in-law, or in another category other than wife. They lived in households whose income was considered adequate, and were located in the lowland zone of the country. These women considered themselves to have no greatest problem in their husbands' absence, which tended to be true of those aged 20 or younger. Next likely to have low strain scores were those wives whose greatest problem was in an area other than agriculture, who tended to be those 25 years old or younger.

They were the group most likely to feel that their husbands continue to make important family decisions while away, and least likely to feel that family fields and livestock are their responsibility in his absence. Freedom from responsibility for agriculture tends to be true of those wives aged 20 or younger, and to a slightly lesser extent, those aged 21 to 25. Daughters-in-law of household heads are least likely to feel this to be their responsibility, closely followed by those related neither as daughter-in-law nor wife.

The High Strain Score Group. The wives experiencing the greatest strain in their husbands' absence were in almost all respects the mirror opposite of those in the low strain score group. It is the older women, with more children, with husbands who have been migrants for longer periods, with a greater likelihood of bearing the responsibility for fields and livestock, who are likely to be having the greatest difficulty. Specifically, wives with the following characteristics were found to be experiencing high levels of strain:

—Those over 25 years old. Those older than this have an even greater chance of having a score in the high range. More than half of the wives over 30 were found to have high scores.
—Those who are the wives of the head of their households.

—Those having four or more children.
—Those married before 1966. Those married before 1956 have an increased chance of having a high strain score, with over 50 per cent of these wives found to have scores in this range.
—Those with husbands at least 26 years old. Those with husbands over 35 have an even greater chance of having a score in the high range.
—Those whose husbands started working as migrants before 1965. Those whose husbands started before 1956, have an even greater probability of having a high strain score, with more than half having scores in the high range.
—Those whose husbands have worked as migrants for more than ten years. Those whose husbands have worked for more than 20 years have an increased chance of having a high strain score, with over 50 per cent having a high score.
—Those whose household income in inadequate.
—Those who live in the mountain zone of the country.
—Those who feel that their greatest problem in their husbands' absence is one related to fields and livestock. This tends to be true of wives over 25 years old, in steadily increasing percentages as age increases. In the over 40 age group, one wife in two cited a problem in this area.
—Those who feel that their husbands do not continue to make important decisions concerning the family while away.
—Those who feel that the family fields and livestock are their responsibility in their husbands' absence, which increases steadily with age. By the 26–30 age group, 86 per cent of the wives feel this to be their responsibility. Wives are also more likely to feel this to be their responsibility (82 per cent) than are daughters-in-law of the head of the household (47 per cent).

DISCUSSION AND CONCLUSIONS

The Wives Experiencing the Greatest Stress

A consideration of the wives identified as experiencing the greatest strain leads to the postulation of three factors[9] that describe it, distinguishing these wives from others with less strain. It is concluded that a process exists by which migrant wives find themselves in positions of increasing difficulty.

First, it is clear that the wives identified as most likely to be in the high strain group are those that tend to have *greater responsibilities*. The fact that they tend to be older, to be the wives of the head of their households, and to have more children would put them in the position of having more problems to solve, dependents to provide for, and responsibilities to meet. Fields and livestock for which the high strain groups tends to see itself responsible, appears to be an especial burden, incurring problems of great concern.

Second, a number of the identifying characteristics point to the wives in this group as tending to be those with *fewer resources* to call upon. The fact that these wives are more likely to be those living in households with inadequate incomes point to their having diminished financial resources. Their greater likelihood of living in the mountain zone of Lesotho means that they have fewer goods and services available to them and greater difficulty with transport and communication than women living in the foothills or lowlands. Also, their greater tendency to have a husband whom they describe as not concerning himself with family problems while away, means that the wives experiencing significant strain are those who cannot rely upon the financial and emotional support of their husbands. These women appear to be impoverished in more ways than one; the financial, emotional and societal resources upon which they are able to draw appear to be less than those of more fortunate women.

The third factor that becomes clear is these women's *longer exposure to their husbands' migration*. The women who are experiencing the greatest strain appear to be those who have lived intimately with the effects of labour migration for the greatest number of years. They tend to be married longer, and to have husbands who have worked as migrants for many years. Whatever the negative effects of the absence of the husband may be, these appear to be exacerbated the longer he is away from home and are not cancelled out by commensurate positive gains. The overall effect is of increasing strain as the years apart lengthen.

It may be seen that the factors that describe the high strain group do not, in the main, set it qualitatively apart from those wives not experiencing the high levels of strain. Rather, the factors that distinguish this group appear to be largely quantitative ones; these women have more responsibilities and fewer resources, and have had longer exposure to labour migration.

As a woman goes through life, it becomes increasingly likely that she will acquire the characteristics found to be associated with high strain. She is likely to move into a position of increased responsibility in her household, to have her available resources outpaced by her responsibilities, and to live apart from her husband for ever-increasing years. The indications are that she will experience significant difficulty as this occurs. Thus, although a wife may not be in a position of considerable strain at present, there is no assurance that she will not find herself in such a position in the future.

Experiencing significant strain, thus, appears to involve a process, in which the wives of migrants become increasingly vulnerable with the years. Rather than an isolated group of women who experience difficulties, every wife has the potential to fall victim to this process, experiencing ever-increasing difficulty as time goes on.

Implications of the Results for the Differing Viewpoints as to Women in this Position

A number of results, both general and specific, are found to be pertinent with regard to existing views on the position of migrants' wives. First, the general view that the wives are placed in a difficult position by their husbands' migration from Lesotho would tend to be supported by this research. The wives with considerable exposure to labour migration appear to be suffering its ill-effects. Those not in considerable difficulty are likely to be those who have simply had less contact with the system. Continued exposure is likely to put them at the same level of strain as the older women.

There are a number of relevant issues which can be discussed in the light of specific results and their bearing on established viewpoints. These will be described below. It can be seen that the viewpoints suggesting the existence of supports from kinsmen, or the creation of a new independence for women were not supported by the present findings.

Migration as a Normal Way of Life to which the Families have been Accustomed

This view posited that the very existence of labour migration in Lesotho, in terms of its long history and widespread prevalence, means that it is not significantly disruptive. Families are described as adjusting to this phenomenon, becoming accustomed to the absence of their men, and functioning without undue difficulty without them.

The findings of the present study would make it difficult to accept such a position. Consistent with this viewpoint would have been results that pointed to the younger women, with the shortest exposure to labour migration, as experiencing greater strain than the older wives. Strain should have decreased as the initial shock of separation lessened and wives became increasingly accustomed to living without their husbands. Greater exposure to labour migration should, according to this view, have meant greater ease of functioning as wives learned to accommodate to their husbands' absence. The results of the present study were consistently in the opposite direction, with the older wives, having had greater exposure to labour migration, experiencing greater strain in their husbands' absence. It thus appears that rather than increased familiarity with the situation leading to a better ability to cope and an adaptation to the husbands' absence, greater exposure leads to greater difficulty. Labour migration and the resultant absence of the husband appear to be influences too disruptive of family life to permit graceful adjustment and accommodation.

The Extended Family as Largely Substituting for the Absent Husband

This view postulated that the effects of labour migration on the family were muted by the extended family fulfilling the functions of the absent husband. Kinsmen were thought to give help and assistance where needed; taking over the absent man's responsibilities, giving social and emotional support to his wife and children, and supervising his fields and livestock. The present study examined a number of variables that pertain directly to this discussion. The first two refer to the wives' raising children in the husbands' absence, the third to responsibility for fields and livestock.

The first variable, was a question asking the wives whether they felt it was important for a father to help bring up his children. Out of 22 attitude questions, this proved to be the one on which the wives were most unanimous, with 94 per cent agreeing on the importance of the father's role. The second relevant question was perhaps more directly to the point, asking whether the wives felt that 'as long as there are other male relatives present to help raise children, it doesn't matter whether the children's father is present'. The majority of the wives did not think that this was true, apparently feeling that a male kinsman was not an adequate substitute for an absent father.

The third question queried whether the wife felt that she bore the responsibility for the family's fields and livestock in her husband's absence. Presumably, if she did not feel this to be the case, she considered this responsibility to rest either with her husband even when away, or with someone other than herself or her husband, presumably another family member. In the present study, 74 per cent of the wives whose families have fields and/or livestock consider this responsibility to be their own. This does not point to kinsmen as largely taking over this function in the husband's absence. In addition, the significant number of wives experiencing high levels of strain associated with responsibility for fields and livestock and considering the greatest difficulty of the wives to be related to fields and livestock, indicates that the extended family does not have a strong impact in this area. Should the wives have had significant aid from their families with these concerns, it is questionable whether more than a third would have described their greatest problem as one related to agriculture and whether responsibility for fields and livestock would have been associated, at an extremely high level of probability, with strain. Any assistance that kinsmen may provide, therefore, appears not to be extensive or effective enough to significantly influence the way in which the wives function or the burden that they bear.

Decision-making Function of Wives and their Attitudes towards it

An additional issue relevant to the views discussed is concerned with whether the wife is the decision-maker in family and property matters in the husband's absence, or whether the husband retains this function. How the wife views this possible decision-making function, as an unwelcome responsibility, or as a positive extension of desired freedom of action, was raised as a related issue.

The findings of the study point to a complex situation with regard to decision-making, but are fairly clear as to the wives' possible enjoyment of this. The results indicate that the wives do feel that they make decisions on family affairs in the absence of their husbands. Sixty-five per cent of the wives stated this to be the case, in response to a question querying this point. At the same time, however, an even larger percentage (78 per cent) felt that their husbands continued to make important decisions concerning the family while away at work. These findings may mean that, rather than acting independently with regard to family affairs, wives tend to make decisions jointly with their husbands. Alternatively, it is possible that husbands and wives have different spheres of family concerns in which they are responsible for decision-making. Or, it may simply be that either the wife or the husband makes the decision, depending on the particular circumstances. In any case, it does not appear that either spouse has the sole responsibility for making important family decisions, but rather that both play a part.

Regarding responsibility for fields and livestock, 74 per cent of the wives consider themselves as bearing this with their husbands away. This result, however, is difficult to interpret in terms of decision-making. Agriculture as it is practised in Lesotho, involves many activities, and different levels of responsibility in decision-making. It is likely, for example, that a wife may have the responsibility for carrying out much of the actual day-to-day work of agriculture, whether doing it herself, or arranging for it to be done. She may, however, have little participation in shaping the long-term decisions regarding agriculture and cattle. Evidence is available to show that it is the husband who retains that function while away, to the extent of punishing his wife severely if his instructions are not followed. Against this background statements asserting that women have largely taken over the responsibility for agriculture in Southern Africa certainly appear to be premature. Research projects need to be designed which examine this complex decision-making process and which carefully delineate the specific roles of husband and wife in the management of agriculture in order to have an accurate picture.

The cross-tabulations of strain scores with variables relating to responsibility and decision-making furnish no evidence that the wives enjoy such functions. Should these functions be viewed positively, it might be expected that women exercising them to a greater degree, would be experiencing less strain. Those women in more responsible positions in their households, i.e. older women, wives rather than daughters-in-law of the household head, should be having less difficulty than those in more dependent positions, because of their greater independence of action. Instead, the findings show that those circumstances likely to bring with them greater decision-making and responsibility were associated with higher, and not lower, levels of strain.

The results of the cross-tabulations with variables that specifically pertain to responsibility and independent decision-making tend to support the same conclusion as regards enjoyment of these functions. In almost every instance, greater responsibility was associated with higher levels of strain. Wives' decision-making in regard to their families was found not to be associated with strain score. It might be argued that should such decision-making be enjoyed, it should be expected to negatively correlate with strain. A striking finding of the study relating to independent decision-making by wives, was the increased likelihood of high strain scores for wives whose absent husbands did not make important decisions concerning the family. Wives who operate without their husbands' input in family matters appear to have significantly more difficulty than those who make such decisions with their husbands' help. Independent decision-making, thus, cannot be seen to be an activity enjoyed by the wives, but rather one associated with unpleasant stress.

There is evidence that responsibility for fields and livestock is, similarly, not enjoyed by the wives. Over a third of the wives described their greatest problem in their husband's absence as agriculture-related, a factor that was associated with strain. Also, those wives who felt they bore this responsibility had a significantly greater likelihood of having a high strain score than did wives who did not consider this responsibility to be theirs. Responsibility in this area of endeavour, within the limits that the wives currently experience it, appears to be felt as a considerable burden, one that is scarcely enjoyed.

It is difficult, therefore, to see the assumption of increased responsibility as being a positive force in these womens' lives. There is data available from an additional question that queried this point directly, asking the wives whether they 'enjoy the independence you get when your husband is away'. Seventy-two per cent of the wives felt that this did not reflect their feelings, with only 28 per cent assenting to this viewpoint.

The view that the wife of an absent migrant is in a significantly difficult position is maintained by the research results. The supports postulated as being available to her in either of the alternative viewpoints, appear not to exist. She appears unable to rely on kinsmen for substantial assistance in those areas of life which are her greatest concerns, and also to lack the personal resources, both emotional and financial, that would permit her to assume and enjoy an independent role.

The Specific Conditions Operative in Lesotho

There appears to be a configuration of factors operating in Lesotho which combine to make the situation especially difficult for the wives of its migrants. These conditions, which create a situation in which it becomes particularly unlikely that kinsmen provide substantial assistance, or that women assume an independent role, serve as a background against which the study's conclusions can be further understood. Speculation as to the salient conditions of life in Lesotho is presented below.

The fact that migration in Lesotho includes such an overwhelming number of men, and comprises so many years of their lives, is seen as creating a number of these conditions. The villages of Lesotho may be almost totally depleted of able-bodied men. The few that are left clearly could not begin to fulfil all the functions of those absent. Moreover, there are such great numbers of women left behind that sympathy for a particular woman's plight may not be forthcoming; a woman left alone is the norm in Lesotho and no compulsion to help her may be felt. The fact that the men's absence from Lesotho often involves fifteen or more years away conceivably also plays a part. Whereas a kinsman might feel some obligation to help a woman left alone for a limited period, he may be hard-pressed to feel such enthusiasm when it means permanently taking her responsibilities upon himself.

Conditions related to the men's work may also contribute to determining the wives' position. The sphere of work appears to be one over which the man exercises little control. A man in Lesotho has little choice but to become a migrant worker, whatever his feelings on the matter. The lack of job opportunities within the country means that there may be no other way he can obtain work. Also, it must be kept in mind that the place to which he migrates is South Africa, and not, as may be true in other settings, an urban area within his own country. His long work years are spent under the humiliating and constraining conditions of apartheid, often in the especially controlled setting of a mine compound. Theoretically, under such adverse conditions, a Basotho migrant might have a special interest in maintaining control over some sphere of his life. The only sphere over which he is able to exert a degree of control may be his family and property back home. It might be speculated, therefore, that a Basotho migrant may be especially likely to insist upon retaining the decision-making function in his family, and upon keeping his wife in a dependent position.

Specific conditions in Lesotho also seem to make the woman's position an especially dependent, passive and stressful one. She appears to have very little control over a number of important areas of her life. She has little say in whether her husband migrates or not. Whether she likes it or not, no matter how badly she may have functioned in his previous absence, she cannot influence this basic condition of her life. She also knows that she has no control over her husband's actions while he is away. The number and frequency of his visits home, his fidelity to her, whether he will choose to completely abandon the family, all lie outside of her control. She is largely dependent on his good-will in these matters.

Income appears to be an especially critical area over which a wife exercises little control. The lack of wage-earning opportunities available means that there is virtually no way she can earn enough money to support herself and her children through her own efforts. There are, in addition, no social welfare programmes to which she can apply for funds. In most cases, therefore, she is left totally dependent on her husband for financial support. When and if he sends money depends upon his own circumstances and motivations. Her income is never assured; when her husband sends money, she has an income, when he does not, she is without.[10] Her often total dependence on her husband for the livelihood may also help to ensure her dependent position in their relationship: it serves to determine power relations within the family – enhancing the husband's ability to control and further eroding her power.

Further, the apparently difficult role women play in family decision-making serves to make their position in the family a stressful one. It appears that she is often given the responsibility for carrying out family affairs according to her husband's orders, and is ultimately accountable to him for her actions. She is likely to undertake this, however, within a framework of little freedom of action, often inadequate expertise, and insufficient resources. (Husbands have been known to neglect to send the money necessary to carry out their own instructions.) To be expected to carry out a task, while realising that a successful completion is probably not possible though one will be held accountable for any failure (and perhaps physically punished for it), is a clearly stressful situation, and one likely to further undermine the wife's self-confidence.

Given these conditions, the existence of an independent position for women in Lesotho can be seen as particularly unlikely. It is difficult to imagine a woman effectively challenging her husband for control of family resources when they both know she is ultimately dependent upon him for her basic subsistence. Perhaps more to the point, it is difficult to think of women presumably conditioned to dependence, passivity, and lack of control as seeing themselves acting independently, and having the confidence and strength of character necessary to take steps directed towards such a goal.

It may be speculated, therefore, that the position of women in Lesotho is especially difficult because of the particular pattern of socio-economic conditions peculiar to Lesotho. Conditions in another country could differ in such a way that the situation of its women might be very different. They might very well find themselves in circumstances where they could actually call upon the supports postulated as being available. Labour migration of a less intense nature, in which fewer men migrated for shorter periods, might mean more help forthcoming for the women left alone. Should conditions of work differ in another setting, such that a man could exert some control over both the job he chooses and his life while on the job, he might not insist on retaining control over his family, and might agree to allow his wife an independent role. Women in a better position to support themselves financially, and with greater self-confidence and control over their lives, would conceivably be more able to demand and assume an independent role.

The conclusions reached in this investigation of women's lives, therefore, must be considered within the framework in which they were reached: the conditions extant in Lesotho. Only further research, investigating the specific conditions operating in other settings, can determine whether they are applicable elsewhere, to women in other countries. It is hoped that this analysis of particular women's lives has served to define issues that might fruitfully be explored, and to stimulate interest in further research directed towards this end.

NOTES

1. This percentage was found in a study of migrants done in conjunction with the present study, and by Van der Wiel [1977:34]. A slightly higher rate, 73 4 per cent, was reported by McDowall [1974] for miners.
2. It is clear that many men never reach retirement, but rather die while still part of the migrant labour system. The rate of attrition is considerable. McDowall [1974] found the death rate per thousand miners to be 3.8 per cent, accident rate 3.8 per cent, occupational diseases of lungs and skin 42.8 per cent, and other illnesses 39.3 per cent. These figures only include accidents and illnesses serious enough to result in termination of employment and repatriation to the home country. The present author's investigation of workmen's compensation cases being handled by the Department of Labour in Lesotho, indicates a higher death rate. It was found that six Basotho miners are killed every month, making a death rate per 1,000 of about 5 per cent.
3. See the following sources for a discussion of the negative effects of labour migration on the family. The first four refer specifically to the situation in Lesotho: Murray [1976], Cobbe [1976], Poulter [1976:20–7], Agency for Industrial Mission [1976], Schlemmer [1976], and Read [1942:605–31].
4. For a detailed description of all aspects of the research method, see Gordon [1978].
5. This was done for purely practical reasons. The wealth of data collected was considerable, and the schedule dictated by the research contract did not permit an analysis which included every interview. As the questionnaires analysed were randomly selected, and were drawn from all sample sites, and so achieved the variability that had been an original concern, no sampling bias was felt to be thus introduced.
6. See Gordon [1978] for a detailed presentation of the research results. Tables of all significant cross-tabulations are included.
7. These are direct translations of questions administered in Sesotho.
8. Wives for whom a question was irrelevant, who gave no answer, or who answered 'don't know' were not included when determining these percentages. Only those with 'yes' and 'no' responses to a question were included, with these considered to add up to 100 per cent.
9. An additional factor found to be characteristic of the wives experiencing the greatest strain was their greater likelihood of favouring alternatives that would allow them to live with their husbands. That is, although the majority of the total sample of wives did not favour living with their husbands at his place of work (40 per cent of the total sample said that they favoured such a possibility), fewer wives in the low strain group (30 per cent) and more in the high strain group (48 per cent) stated this as their preference. Similarly, although the great majority of the total sample (92 per cent), favoured their husbands' working in Lesotho, a lower percentage of the low strain group agreed with this attitude (84 per cent), and an overwhelming 97 per cent of the high strain group felt that this reflected their view.
10. See Gordon [in press] for details as to how the families of migrants obtain their income.

REFERENCES

Agency for Industrial Mission, ed., 1976, 'Another Blanket: Report of an Investigation into the Migrant Situation', A. I. M. Horizon.

Berg, Elliot J., 1965, 'The Economics of the Migrant Labour System', in Kuper, Hilda, ed., *Urbanization and Migration in West Africa*, Berkeley: University of California Press.

Clarke, Liz and Ngobese, Jane, 1975, *Women Without Men*, Durban: Institute for Black Research.

Cobbe, J. H., 1976, 'Approaches to Conceptualization and Measurement of the Social Costs of Labour Migration from Lesotho', in Agency for Industrial Mission, ed., *South Africa Today: A Good Host Country for Migrant Workers?* (mimeo).

Colson, Elizabeth, 1970, 'Family Change in Contemporary Africa', in Middleton, John, ed., *Black Africa*, London: Macmillan.

Gay, Judy, undated, 'Women Without Men: Female Social Networks in a Male Controlled Society'. (mimeo).

Gordon, Elizabeth, 1978, *The Women Left Behind: A Study of the Wives of the Migrant Workers of*

Lesotho, Geneva, ILO, December, mimeographed World Employment Programme research working paper (WEP 2–26/WP 35).

Gordon, Elizabeth, in press, 'Proposals for Easing the Plight of Migrant Workers' Families in Lesotho', in Böhning, W. R., ed., *Black Migration to South Africa*, Geneva: ILO.

McDowall, M., 1974, 'Basotho Labour in South African Mines – an Empirical Study' (mimeo, unpaged), November.

Moody, Elize, 1976, 'Women and Development in South Africa', *Development: Southern African Edition*, (3), pp. 26–9.

Murray, Colin, 1976, *Keeping House in Lesotho: A Study of the Impact of Oscillating Migration*, unpublished Ph.D. thesis, University of Cambridge.

Murray, Colin, 1976, 'Marital Strategy in Lesotho: the Redistribution of Migrant Earnings', *African Studies*, 35:2, pp. 99–121.

Nattrass, Jill, 1975, 'The Migrant Labour System and South Africa's Economic Development', Department of Economics, University of Natal, September, (mimeo).

Poulter, Sebastian, 1976, *Family Law and Litigation in Basotho Society*, Oxford: Clarendon Press.

Read, Margaret, 1942, 'Migrant Labour in Africa and its Effects on Tribal Life', *International Labour Review*, XLV:6, pp. 605–31.

Schlemmer, Lawrence, 1976, 'Social and Cultural Perspectives on Migratory Labour', in Agency for Industrial Mission, ed. *South Africa Today: A Good Host Country for Migrant Workers?* (mimeo, unpaged).

Spiegel, Andrew, 1975, *Christian Marriage and Migrant Labour in a Lesotho Village*, unpublished B.A. thesis, University of Cape Town.

Spiegel, Andrew, 1975, 'Christianity, Marriage and Migrant Labour in Lesotho', in Verryne, T. D., ed., *Church and Marriage in Modern Africa*, Groenkloof: Ecumenical Research Unit.

Van der Wiel, A. C. A., 1977, *Migratory Wage Labour: Its Role in the Economy of Lesotho*, Mazenod: Mazenod Book Centre.

Williams, John C., 1971, 'Lesotho: Economic Implications of Migrant Labour', *The S.A. Journal of Economics*, 39:2, pp. 149–78.

Perspectives in Development: The Problem of Nurses and Nursing in Zambia

by Ilsa Schuster

The training of indigenous women in hospital nursing is directly modelled on western services. Hence training does not address social problems attendant on implicit cultural conflict between indigenous and western healing systems and conceptualisations of illness. Because these problems are not faced in the curriculum, nurses are imperfectly socialised into the modern health care setting. They, and the public, continue to accept the efficacy of both health care systems, assuming complementarity when in fact in many respects they conflict. The involvement of young women in healing, a radical innovation, became institutionalized. Because of the high visibility of the nurse and a radical change in the role of young women as healers, and because of the vulnerability of the patients, conflict in treatment systems focused on nurses who became scapegoats in hospitals, which came to be called 'houses of death'.

INTRODUCTION

Since Boserup's seminal work [*1970*] demonstrating that colonialism and initial development efforts undermined the traditional position of women and increased their economic marginality in the modern economic sector, the importance of involving women in development has become widely recognised by international development agencies and Third World policy-makers. The USAID now distinguishes between women-specific projects and women's components in general projects [*1978:2–3*]. The foci of interest in development projects, whether women-specific or containing women's components, are becoming oriented toward rural income generation [*Nelson, 1979*]. Less attention has been paid to the process of indigenisation of institutional frameworks inherited from the colonial past. As such institutions expand in the post-independence era, indigenous women become 'natural' recruits to systems in which colonial or other expatriate women were employed [*Schuster, 1979b*]. Involving women in development thus comes to mean two analytically separate processes: creating new forms of work in the traditional sector [*Schuster, 1979a*], and replacing foreigners with indigenes in the modern sector.

The development of nursing services is an example of the latter. Most Third World countries inherited from their colonial past at least the skeleton of modern health service facilities, usually no less than a hospital in the capital city and a few mission hospitals in the rural hinterland. Paralleling other high technology institutions in the modern sector, these medical cultural imports from the mother country were conceived and operated almost exclusively by expatriates. Local citizens were mostly employed in unskilled maintenance work. When independence increased the impetus for further expansion and development of health service facilities, indigenous women became the 'natural' recruits for nursing. The active recruitment of women as nurses parallels their recruitment as typists, stenographers, primary school teachers, air hostesses – occupations which are classically associated with females in the west. This transfer is part of a larger cultural process of imitation that Mazrui [1978] defines as the perpetuation of cultural dependency, of which economic dependency is a part.

The notion of what one might call 'medical dependency' has recently been challenged along the dimensions of relevancy to primary, preventive health needs in the Third World. Enquiries tend to follow one of two themes. One theme is the relationship between traditional medical concepts and practices and the concepts and practices of the newly established or expanded medical system developed on the western model. Analyses may include the roles of traditional and western healers, and the advisability or inadvisability of integrating the two systems [Asuni, 1979; Imperato, 1979; Kleinman, 1978; Gish, 1979; Taylor, 1979]. The other theme concerns the various problems of setting up or reforming health care systems in Third World countries. Analyses have pointed out the trend common in the Third World to emphasise more the curative, urban-teaching hospital oriented medical programme than the preventive primary care programme. Sometimes analyses relate the trend to a variety of factors: the political ideology of the country, its political economy, the western training of its indigenous physicians, or to the problems involved in changing the orientation [Bossert 1979 a, b; Bryant, 1969; King, 1966; Joseph, 1979; Mburu, 1979].

The problem of nurses and nursing in developing countries has received scant attention in the literature on medicine and social science or the development of medical services. Physicians sensitive to social issues [King, 1966; Bryant, 1969] have limited their analyses to the planning of schools of nursing, the role of the nurse as a member of a health care team, and the reasons why professional nurses working in Third World countries often have greater responsibilities for health care than do nurses working in developed countries.[1] These physicians are sensitive to the need for training that is relevant. As Herskovitz pointed out long ago [1962, 230–1], the idea of educational relevance is not new. Relevancy was an issue even in colonial educational policies. Contemporary social scientists [Frankenburg, 1969; Mazrui, 1978] continue to appeal for it, usually by suggesting the introduction of courses in anthropology, sociology and psychology to health service students. That relevancy continues to remain a hotly debated issue in modernisation and development is evidence of the complex nature of the problem. As for other aspects of nurses and nursing in the Third World, such as their social problems in and out of the medical facility, the literature is sparse indeed. An outstanding contribution is Kuper's study [1965] of the relationship of nursing to the ideology of apartheid and the impact on nurses in the hospital and beyond its walls in South Africa. South Africa can hardly be called a developing country in the sense we normally use the term. There are similarities in some of the problems faced by black South African nurses and nurses elsewhere in black Africa, but apartheid creates a maze of unique problems that arises in far milder form, if at all, elsewhere.

Despite differences in philosophies of development, and despite the wide range of theoretical orientations in the literature on the roles of women in development and the development of health care facilities, there is a virtual consensus that the work of professional nursing is vital no matter what the orientation of the health care system, and that young women in preference to young men should be trained as professional nurses.

Historically, western female nurses fought a long, hard battle for respectability. Over the years, the western nurse has won a positively valued social position as a symbolic extension of the services performed by a warmly soothing, nurturant mother easing her family's pain. The 'lady with the lamp', the 'angel of mercy', has come into her own, and nursing has developed a distinctive point of view in its specific, continuous professional concern for the comfort and well-being of people [*Bryant, 1969*; *Brink, 1979*].[2] It is no accident that 'Florence Nightingale' has come into common linguistic usage as an epithet for altruism. The very success of nursing as a female profession is witnessed by the assumption in most non-western countries that nurses should 'naturally' be women. It does not follow, however, that the young women recruited to nurse-training programmes in countries of the Third World fit into the western cultural paradigm, either in terms of their own motivations to enter professional training, or in terms of their reception as nurses by their societies. There may be instead serious problems of culture clash.

This paper concerns the problems of nurses and nursing in Zambia, a central African republic which gained independence from Great Britain in 1964.[3] Zambia presents a cultural setting in which there is no traditional association of healing with young women, and where nursing in modern medical facilities in the colonial period was a white female preserve. In their total acceptance of western health service models, development planners established nurse training programmes for young Zambian women. Beginning with a brief look at the social context of the programme, the paper contrasts the social backgrounds, expectations, and hospital experiences of the recruits with their reception by society at large. My hypothesis is that the complete acceptance by planners of a western model of health care creates conflict between Zambian and western social and cultural concepts of illness and healing. These conflicts are focused on the new young recruits to the nursing profession. As a result, their position in society, as the first generation of locally trained nurses, is fraught with ambivalence. Student nurses internalise this ambivalence and it influences their response to society at large, including patients. Cultural clashes cause tension in the hospital atmosphere, heightened by the overburdening of medical facilities, itself a function of the acceptance of western treatment by the wider society.

I further suggest that the problems of nurses are a manifestation of the wider problem of a first generation of women educated beyond the level generally available to the masses. Education opens up employment opportunities, contributing to the sudden, unprecedented rise in women's positions, and evoking the ambivalent response to the new subelite urban women by society at large. The issues around which ambivalence focuses vary according to the nature of the occupation; the underlying processes are the same.

THE ESTABLISHMENT OF NURSE TRAINING PROGRAMMES: THE WIDER CONTEXT

Health care in Zambia in the colonial period reflected a duality that developed in the economic sector. In the latter, a modern western industrial sector was created around the mineral rich deposits in the north of the country, and European planned towns developed along the north-south line of rail. The rest of the country was a largely underdeveloped labour reserve. Health care services followed a similar principle. The colonial government and the mining companies established modern western-type hospitals in the urban sector. Private 'fee-paying' hospitals were intended for the resident white community, separate free hospitals, staffed by white professional personnel, for the Africans. Christian missions established rural hospital facilities for Africans. The majority of the African population, both in the rural labour reserves and in towns, relied upon traditional methods of treating illness, and were rarely able to use modern facilities.

Throughout the colonial period, the training of Africans in western medical techniques was almost totally neglected, although missions made sporadic and painfully small-scale efforts to train male medical assistants and female nurses' aides. There were no training programmes at a professional level for African doctors or nurses. Zambian secondary school graduates wishing to undertake university studies or nursing training went abroad. In the early 1960s an occasional graduate of the best secondary school for girls, Chipembe, attended the School of Nursing at Mpilo Hospital in Bulawayo, Rhodesia (now Zimbabwe). After finishing the three year course, she could go to Salisbury, Rhodesia's capital, for a midwifery course.[4] So rare was this route to professional nurse training that the *Survey of Occupations in 1969* (p. 41), published by Zambia's Central Statistical Office lists no professional Zambian African nurses and only 25 nurses' aides.

Before independence, there were few problems of culture clash between western and indigenous systems of medical care, and virtually no social problem for young women seeking professional training, since the available western health care was extremely limited and there were no opportunities for young women to enter any sort of training programme, either in health services or in anything else. Young women were expected to marry. As rural wives they were expected to farm; as urban wives they were expected to keep house. The notion that urban women might work in unskilled employment, for example in market trade, met with such resistance by men − and some women − that few women attempted to work outside the home [*Schuster, 1979a*]. As late as five years after independence, the *Survey of Occupations in 1969* (p. 41) lists only 583 Zambian African women employed throughout the country, against 37,075 males employed. From the women's perspective, problems with their position in the colonial period were very basic indeed: whether to migrate to town or remain in the rural area, how to survive in town as a dependent on an unreliable male income, and what to do and where to go when that form of support was not forthcoming.

The notion that the limited available formal western education was wasted on young girls was widespread. This attitude was relatively realistic, given the absence of employment opportunity [*Schuster, 1979b*]. The idea that a young Zambian girl could be a professional nurse seemed remote because so few Africans experienced western medical care, and because all professional doctors and nurses were white. Even after nursing programmes were established becoming a nurse was not a common aspiration. In my study of women's aspirations, 50 housewives in a Lusaka shanty town were asked if they wanted their daughters to work, and what sort of jobs they would like their daughters to have. Nearly all preferred that their daughters work for a few years before marrying, but not one mentioned nursing as a desired occupation.

Following independence, the Zambian government embarked upon a programme of radical socio-economic change, which it hoped would have a permanent impact on all aspects of the lives of its rural and urban citizens. Under the guiding egalitarian political ideology of 'Humanism', [*Meebelo, 1973*], it aimed at improving the quality of life and achieving a western standard of living for all Zambians by developing mechanisms by which western skills could be mastered and western technology transferred. The overall conception of development was therefore overwhelmingly western. This western conceptualisation of planning included the organisation of specific development projects and the training of manpower to replace foreign personnel in existing work situations and to fill new jobs in an expanding economy. Thus the general context of national development included expanding primary and secondary educational facilities, opening a university which included the same types of schools found in the west (Humanities, Sciences, Law, Engineering, Medicine), creating a university teaching hospital, [*Mwanakatwe, 1968*] establishing training facilities for numerous types of skilled work in urban training centres, (*Zambian Manpower, 1969*), expanding and diversifying industry (*Second National Development Plan 1971*; cf. [*Seidman, 1974*]), and finally, expanding all types of medical facilities and establishing a nation-wide network of health services [*Statistical Year Book, 1971:17*]. The dynamic of the pattern was to assess a need in a particular region of the country – for a school, a factory, a hospital, a clinic – build it, and import foreign personnel to run it while training Zambians to eventually take over.

The government allocated funds for the building of new hospitals and the expansion of existing government, mission, and private hospitals, health centres and clinics in both urban and rural areas. Between 1964 and 1971 there was a 52 per cent increase in the number of full-time health centres and clinics (from 306 to 556). This expansion created serious professional manpower shortages. In 1964, for example, an estimated 639 foreign nurses were employed in Zambia's hospitals. By 1969 the number had increased to 1,145 [*Statistical Year Book, 1970:12*]. By 1972 estimates of the shortfall of nurses ranged widely from 600 to 2,666; in that year efforts were made, with little success, to recruit 400 nurses from Britain, the West Indies, India and Swaziland.[5]

In the context of rapid development of medical facilities and difficulty of recruiting foreign professional nurses, there was enormous pressure to produce local nurses. Between 1965 and 1973 four schools were established for professional nurse training. Recruits to these three year programmes, leading to a diploma as a State Registered Nurse, are graduates of Form Five of secondary school. In the initial development period, the government depended on the private sector – mines and mission hospitals – to train practical nurses. Practical nurses are Form Two graduates with ten years of schooling recruited for a two-year course leading to a diploma as an Enrolled Nurse. The government intends eventually to build facilities to train practical nurses in the various provincial capitals: Mongu, Chipata, Kasama, Mansa and Kitwe, as well as the Copperbelt town of Kabwe and in Lusaka, the capital.

The first government school of nursing for the three-year programme was located at the Kitwe Central Hospital in the Copperbelt town of Kitwe, had a capacity for training 100 students and, in 1968, an enrollment of 90. That year construction started on the Lusaka University Teaching Hospital, whose school of nursing was opened in 1969, with an initial intake of 25 and an eventual capacity of about 300. The Roan Consolidated Mining Company began a school in its hospital in the Copperbelt town of Mufulira in 1970. By 1972, 150 students were enrolled. The fourth school was opened in late 1973 in the hospital of the Copperbelt town of Ndola. Thus, all schools were established in urban hospitals, none in rural areas. The necessity of urban residence for trainees and the pressure to work within and eventually replace foreigners had important consequences in student perceptions of their social position. The distinction between practical and professional nursing, copied from the west, had important consequences for academic success.

THE SOCIAL BACKGROUNDS OF NURSING STUDENTS

Student nurses grew up in the last phase of the colonial period, entering adolescence at the dawn of independence. In the colonial period, Europeans were the elites, Asians were a middle group, and Africans were at the bottom of the social order. Africans were differentiated according to their education and employment, but the level of African advancement was depressed by a colour bar, the absence of opportunities for further training within the country, and low salary scales. Those Africans who lived in towns or in 'urban enclaves' in the rural areas – mission stations or government centres – and were employed in semi-skilled or sometimes even unskilled occupations or who owned small shops, were the elite within the African group. In contrast, most unskilled workers moved in and out of urban wage employment; most rural village horticulturalists farmed at the subsistence level, few marketing cash crops. The African elites were a transitional generation. No longer traditional rural subsistence farmers, they had limited access to modern life but had developed a modernising outlook.

Students of nursing tend to be children of this transitional generation. The majority grew up in the rural areas, but not in traditional village settings. Rather, they were raised in the urban enclaves. In this protected environment they attended school, their fathers worked for the whites, and their mothers attended homecraft training centres or even worked themselves. Rigid racial segregation removed them and their parents from the possibility of informal social contacts with whites and an intimate understanding of white people's work and life styles, but at the same time the urban life-style provided an awareness of the physical ease and material standards of white life. With the ferment of agitation for independence and its subsequent achievement came rising expectations, especially those of people in towns and in the urban enclaves in the rural areas, who were directly involved in agitating for socio-political change and economic opportunity. The seemingly impossible had become possible. Africans were able to enter white occupations, or to have their children do so.

Table I shows the percentage of interviewees whose childhood and adolescence was spent in rural and urban areas respectively. The majority, 65 per cent, were born and spent their early childhood before primary school in the rural areas. Of these 82 per cent lived in urban enclaves. An additional 3 per cent left the urban areas to attend rural secondary school.

TABLE 1

RURAL/URBAN EARLY CHILDHOOD EXPERIENCE OF 51 STUDENT NURSES

	Urban %	Rural %
Birthplace	35	65
Before primary school	35	65
Primary school	32	68
Secondary school	26	74

The significance of these statistics can be appreciated if we compare the student nurses to less educated, less 'westernised' women of Lusaka of comparable age.[7] Thus, 35 per cent urban is a relatively high percentage for the colonial period when the student nurses were young children. In comparison, among Lusaka's market women interviewees, 16.6 per cent were urban-born; 83.3 per cent born in rural areas.[8] The market women came to town at an earlier age: 38 per cent spent their childhood in urban areas; 54 per cent in rural areas, and 8 per cent alternated between urban and rural areas. But the urban residence of the marketeers did not enhance their educational opportunities; for 42 per cent had no education, 52 per cent had some primary education, and only 6 per cent had some secondary education. None completed secondary school. The chances of completing education were greater if the girl remained in the rural area, for urban schools were overcrowded, and urban children were tempted by street life. While on the whole rural education is inferior to urban education, rural children are more isolated from the temptations of non-schoolgoing peers. Furthermore many of the student nurses – 36 per cent – came from rural Barotseland (Western Province), which has the oldest educational system for Africans in Zambia.[9]

Table II shows sociological indices of the modern outlook of the transitional generation. By 'modern outlook' is meant the awareness of opening opportunities for education and employment, as would be expected of people introduced, however peripherally, to western life. Nearly all fathers (84 per cent) and more than half the mothers (56 per cent) were wage earners. In stark contrast, only 39 per cent of the marketwomen's fathers and 17 per cent of their mothers were wage earners. More than half the nurses' fathers were in skilled employment: 36 per cent in skilled jobs and 28 per cent as self-employed businessmen. As employees they worked primarily as clerks in town or in local government centres, as civil servants or civil servant rural chiefs. A few worked as teachers, clergymen and miners. The father of one nursing student was a medical assistant. Only 16 per cent of the nurses' fathers were unskilled labourers, and another 16 per cent were subsistence farmers. In contrast, 38 per cent of the marketwomen's fathers were unskilled labourers or miners, 59 per cent were susbsistence farmers, and only 2 per cent were in skilled employment. A few of the nurses' mothers were involved in teaching other women in welfare and homecraft centres: still others worked as marketeers. Some helped run their husbands' shops and a number earned money by brewing beer. The few mothers of marketwomen who worked were all themselves either marketwomen or beer brewers. A high percentage of the nursing students – 78 per cent – had female relatives other than their mothers in employment, which indicates that favourable attitudes towards women's achievement were supported in their extended families. Extended family support for young female achievers played an important part in their introduction and socialisation into town life. Most student nurses spent their adolescence in rural boarding schools. In their early boarding school years they would return to their parents' homes at school holiday time. Later on they would travel to towns to be hosted by urban relatives. Nearly all – 99 per cent – had urban relatives and 71 per cent were hosted by these relatives, usually during late adolescence. Thirteen per cent were 'true children of the city', having no contact with the rural areas.

TABLE 2

INDICES OF NURSING STUDENT 'MODERN OUTLOOK'

	%
Father as wage earner	84
Mother as a wage earner	56
Female relatives as wage earners	78
Relatives living in large towns	99
Rural dwellers contact with regional centres	82
Hosted by urban relatives	71
No rural experience	13

Their lives as young girls and adolescents supported the development of a modern outlook in nursing students, expressed as a desire to remain in school and eventually to be the pioneering generation of Zambian working women. But whereas their youthful experiences prepared them to aspire to upward social mobility, they were unprepared for the specific focus on nursing. Counselled by school advisors, graduates applied to several different training programmes, listing their preferences, and would go to the programme into which they were accepted. Acceptance into a preferred programme was a matter of having the right grades for the right programme. Government met all costs of education, but students lacked freedom of choice in training: once given a place it was difficult to change. A girl might want to be a nurse, for example, but because of her high grades she would be assigned to the Bachelor of Science quota at the University, and be required to enter university studies. For many, nursing was not a first choice, but was the only programme into which they were accepted.

Few applicants to the nursing programme had a clear idea of the type of work nurses did. They had limited exposure to modern medical settings. As children, when they became ill, they were normally treated with traditional healing techniques; more rarely they were taken to western medical clinics. Only 8 per cent had themselves been hospital patients at some point in their lives.

To a limited extent, they may have come to nursing with personal experience in caring for the sick, for as young girls they were expected to take care of small children. As soon as a toddler is weaned, he is 'assigned' to a young girl who becomes his nanny. Often toddlers fall ill from the shock of weaning and the drastic change in diet, and the young nanny is expected to care for them. No blame is attached to her should the toddler weaken and die, however. In the case of nursing students, the time spent attending boarding school kept even these limited nursing experiences minimal. They knew little about nursing except that nurses wore attractive uniforms, gave injections, had relatively high monthly salaries, and lived in town where they could enjoy urban leisure activities. They knew that the high social position they would be achieving would provide an introduction to elite and subelite men among whom they would hope to find a husband.

Many relatives with personal experience of hospital settings were opposed to the young women entering nursing. Nursing, they said, was 'dirty' work. Lacking an alternative, however, girls entered into nurse training despite the warnings of relatives. Concerned relatives were seen as restricting a girl's freedom, so their reservations were interpreted as intergenerational conflict between conservative elders and modern young people.

Having a modern outlook therefore, meant that the benefits of western life were appreciated even if the inner content of western culture and institutions were not understood. The culture of the transitional generation and of its daughters who were to train as nurses was Zambian in content, with a superficial addition of some western cultural elements and skills.

This system of thought, values, attitudes and beliefs was rooted in Zambian tradition. This was especially true of concepts of illness and healing. Conceptually, the western medical model and western concepts of health care are in opposition to traditional Zambian ideas. The western model analyses the cause of the breakdown of bodily functioning on the basis of the intrusion or influence of factors in the physical environment. While the social environment may create conditions conducive to illness, it is not the essential cause. The Zambian model does the opposite. The essential cause of bodily malfunction must be sought in the social environment: specifically in the moral order.[10] The breakdown of normal bodily functioning is the result of the violation (deliberately or unwittingly) of the moral universe by some person, either the victim, an enemy, friend, spouse, or relative. All illness is therefore fundamentally spiritual. The victim must be brought afresh into harmony with the social and spiritual order of the community, and indeed, the universe. The method used is to expose the social-spiritual cause of the breakdown or to remove the person from a particular social environment.

Understanding this conceptual opposition was unnecessary for Zambians who would willingly utilise any medical techniques thought to aid the healing process. Rather than seeing the western and traditional systems as opposed to one another, they are seen as complementary, and sometimes necessary for a full cure. If traditional medical procedures are not contraindicated by western procedures, or if they are not used simultaneously, they may coexist without harm. Should they be contraindicated, people must be convinced to choose either one or the other system. Since young girls enter nurse training fresh out of school, they cannot be expected to understand the subtle conceptual differences between these systems. They share with other members of their society the notion of complementarity. Most young students of nursing have experiences, either personal or in their families, in which the effectiveness of traditional procedures over western procedures is demonstrated to their satisfaction. One student said:

The auntie I lived with before coming to the hospital had had headaches for some months. She went to the clinic and got medicines but they did not help. She returned to the clinic five or six times, then two times to a private doctor. He failed to help her. The headaches got worse. Finally she went to an African doctor. He said the cause of her illness was the jealousy of her husband's mother who wanted her husband to marry a woman of their own tribe. He gave her special African medicines to keep her husband's love. He told her that she must cut off some of her hair and bury it in the crossroads near her house at midnight. Then she would give her troubles to the first person who passed at the place where her hair was buried. I don't know how it worked; there are many things I do not understand. But auntie's headaches went away after that. European medicine does not always work better than our African medicines. This is what I know because I have seen it.

Daughters of the transitional generation must not only be educated in western concepts, treatment and procedures, they must also be socialised into accepting the role of nurse. They must accept the notion, foreign to their own culture and experience, that young women have a specific and important role in the healing process.

PROBLEMS WITH THE NURSE TRAINING PROGRAMME

The conceptualisation, planning and development of schools of nursing followed the broad pattern of establishing western institutional structures and training local people in the skills required to serve these institutions irrespective of the suitability to local conditions of trainees and programmes. Despite the early planners' sensitivity to the need for suitability [King, 1966; Frankenberg, 1969], problems arose in recruitment and programme development.

Basic to the problem of planning were the implications of building up a system from a baseline of zero. Nursing schools competed with other programmes for secondary school graduates of Forms Two to Five. Lacking students, some nursing programmes only grew on paper. In the authority's haste to fill vacant places, students who would have preferred training as teachers, secretaries, social workers and air hostesses were assigned to nursing. Many entered nurse training with no science background.

An Act of Parliament, directives from the Ministry of Health, and the reports of the supervisory Zambia Nursing Council set unrealistic western standards for nursing schools. Thus, an 1965 Act of Parliament decreed that recruits to the three-year programme spend two years in course work and a third year in practical lessons in the wards. The Act ignored manpower shortages in hospital staffing that would necessitate student nurses working in the wards. The programme at one hospital was threatened with closure because it required too much ward work for students and not enough classroom work. The structural separation of practical and professional nursing based on a Ministry of Health directive was rigid in setting differential standards but came to be fudged in practice. Thus Form Five graduates who enrolled in the threatened three-year programme were informed in their third year of study that they would be awarded the less valued diploma in Practical Nursing. School authorities, defending the professional level of training as comparable to the other two programmes then available in the country, were locked in conflict with the Ministry. The Ministry advised the angry students to apply to one of the other programmes if they were interested in getting professional nursing diplomas.[11] This suggestion ignored the manpower problems that would be created at the hospital if 150 students were actually to leave its wards. It also ignored the lack of facilities in the other two hospitals to receive large numbers of students in mid-training.

The emotionally-based political decision to maintain strict standards of international excellence in curriculum design created two problems. One was that no remedial courses were offered to students with deficient secondary education, because it was feared academic programmes would be watered down. Just as many students were unprepared for their studies, programmes were equally unprepared to meet their academic deficiencies. Because their individual differences were ignored and they were taught as a group, the rate of failure was inevitably high. Thus the problem became high trainee drop out rates at the same time that the need for new nurses was growing as a result of the expansion of services.[12] A second problem was the failure in curriculum design to compare, contrast and evaluate western and traditional concepts of illness and healing and to examine subcultural differences in Zambian traditional medical practices. It was assumed that when students learned the scientific western cultural paradigm they would no longer accept traditional medical models. In the absence of a serious confrontation with traditional healing, students, only a generation removed from village life, retained their traditional beliefs. They could accept the efficacy of western medical procedures and learn by rote their own new role using these procedures. But lacking a deeper understanding, they would not develop adequate motivation to strictly adhere to western hospital norms when unsupervised.

PROBLEMS IN THE HOSPITAL

In the initial development period, national political leaders expected that by allocating funds unsparingly for the most up-to-date buildings, equipment and training programmes, Zambia would soon have a medical service comparable to that of the developed countries. The abolition of fee-paying hospitals and the establishment of a free medical service available to all the residents of the country, consistent with Humanism, were intended to improve national health standards. The political leadership saw as its function in this regard the encouragement of all citizens to make use of the health services. In this it was highly successful as people flocked to the hospitals and clinics. The University Teaching Hospital in Lusaka was especially popular. People travelled hundreds of kilometres to use its facilities, even when local mission hospitals could have served their medical needs.

Within two or three years, the hospital service came under attack:

There are no sufficiently horrifying adjectives to describe what the Minister of Health found at what is supposed to be the pride and joy of our medical services in this country – the University Teaching Hospital.

After being told of some of the most diabolical behaviour that ... has ever disgraced the wards of any hospital in the world, we can forgive those who are now branding the place as something of a 'chamber of horrors'. [*Times of Zambia, 11 September, 1971*].

The editorial reflects widespread attitudes in society at large. In just a few years after opening its expanded facilities the hospital developed the reputation of being a house of death rather than of healing. The cause, it was said, was the improper care given to patients, and the onus of responsibility was put on the Zambian nursing staff. It was said that people died because they were turned away by nurses, that many of those admitted died for lack of proper nursing care. The simple physical needs of patients were neglected: for hours they would be left unattended, bloody and soiled, while nurses took tea breaks. Busy socialising amongst themselves and their favourite patients, nurses were accused of not properly supervising unskilled ward attendants, who would steal the patients' food. Only the physicians were exempted from the accusation of reporting to work drunk. Nurses were accused of ill-treating patients – of slapping, shouting, and arguing with them. They were labelled irresponsible, negligent, insensitive, arrogant. In their treatment of visitors they were accused of being harsh and rude.[13] The Women's branch of UNIP, the national ruling party, campaigned to stop Zambian nurses from studying midwifery, which had become a popular aspiration for many nursing students wishing to take advanced training.[14]

Clearly, the hospital faced serious problems. There was a measure of truth to the charges against the hospital in general and the nurses in particular. Something had gone awry as the gap between society's expectations and the performance of the hospital seemed to widen. The underlying cause was culture clash which focused on Zambian nurses and nursing students. A number of different issues were involved.

One form that culture clash took was in variations in expectations of nurses. Members of different social strata had different ideas about the role of the Zambian nurse. Educated elite patients shared with the hospital administration the idea that nurses were western-trained personnel working in a western institution, who should be working in a western manner, offering a western standard of service and following western norms of health care. Whereas their rote learning of specific techniques and procedures enabled the nurses to provide such service in theory, they could not provide the attention deemed proper by elites due to staff shortages. But staff shortages at times served as an excuse for inadequate or inefficient work habits, and for the intrusion of other criteria into the nurses' decisions to attend more or less adequately only to particular patients. The basic western premise of medical care is the scientifically based impersonal curative ministrations of doctors and nurses. Despite this, patients in the west may be socially evaluated, and these evaluations by medical staff may affect treatment. In Zambia, evaluations are based on sex, tribe, education and social position.[15] Because of the large number of patients relative to staff, the differentials in treatment can be potentially greater and the results of neglect more severe than in the west.

To unmarried nurses, the most desirable patient is a subelite or elite male.

Despite his temporary medical problem, he is a potential boyfriend. An elite informant spent several months in the hospital suffering multiple fractures. I was a frequent visitor. In the early weeks of his hospitalisation, he reported with amusement how his room was filled with nurses offering constant services. He said that since he and his wife were of different ethnic groups, nurses who sought to attend him were also of various ethnic groups. As weeks went by and his disinterest in developing personal relationships became apparent, nurse visits to his room lessened and eventually stopped, except for one or two nurses from his own ethnic group who were not assigned to his case. He claimed that he would have been almost totally neglected if not for their interest in their tribesman. He wondered if his tribeswomen were neglecting their own patients from other ethnic groups to attend him, and if the allocation of nurse-patient responsibility evened out in the long run if most of the nurses looked after their own tribespeople rather than their assigned case loads.

The problem of caring for uneducated patients was that, as young Zambian women, the nurses did not command the authority to do their jobs. In general, patient evaluations of Zambian nurses have a negative impact on the nurses, putting them in a difficult position. Patients bring to the hospital their own cultural evaluations of the proper behavioural roles of young unmarried Zambian women. Patients may be prepared to accept nursing ministrations of foreign nurses that they would find offensive and try to refuse from Zambians. Precisely because the foreign nurses *are* foreign, they are outside the Zambian moral universe. The Zambian patient can therefore accept treatment and obey instructions of the foreign nurse because these are as impersonal to the patient as to the nurse. The Zambian nurse commands less authority, because she is young and female and Zambian. Sometimes in order to get patients to comply with her orders, the Zambian nurse has no choice except to command. She must cope with expressions of embarrassment and hostility by patients who are in a relationship to her that is new to both parties in the interaction. Physical ministrations to elders embarrass the patients. The position of authority of the Zambian nurse violates a basic premise in Zambian thoughts of respect. The campaign of the UNIP Women's Brigade to forbid young Zambian nurses from attending women in childbirth because this was 'disgraceful and contrary to traditional values'[16] is to be understood in this context.

In her new role as student nurse, the young unmarried woman violates traditional rules of etiquette and modesty in a deeper and more threatening way than do young women in urban occupations that are more morally neutral. Thus, for example, office work and schoolteaching are modern urban occupations that are morally neutral in themselves; others such as vegetable trading and cleaning are extensions of legitimate traditional female domestic activities of food production and home care. But the idea that a young unmarried woman should help the sick is a radical departure from traditional modes of thought about healing and about the role of young women.

At the same time, the nurse's lack of authority was used against her. Thus, in the wards nurses were accused of not respecting patient needs for modesty by not clearing out non-essential personnel when administering treatments. It often happened that attendants would watch a nurse perform a medical procedure. The nurses' acquiescence to the attendants' presence would lend legitimacy, so the patient would not feel free to protest his resentment at the intrusion. Nurses felt they could not do two jobs at once: to keep curious attendants away and administer to patients. If, as a nurse, she ordered attendants to leave the scene, she would be violating a Zambian cultural norm in which young women are never in such positions of command. If she exercised her role as nurse and so ordered them, she opened herself to charges of arrogance and might well be disobeyed. Rather than risk humiliation herself, she humiliated the patient.

The views of uneducated patients toward Zambian nurses were not wholly negative, but were rather, ambivalent. Patients and their visitors expected a degree of heightened communication and understanding between themselves and the Zambian nurses because of their shared languages and cultural backgrounds. Yet this too caused problems for the nurses, for it was they who most directly bore the brunt of the crush of people seeking treatment as in- and out-patients, and the relatives and friends accompanying or visiting patients. Since foreign doctors and nurses did not speak local languages, Zambian nurses had the major responsibility for directing the flow of human traffic – dealing with both patients and the public, attending patients for many hours waiting for doctors to arrive. Charges of rudeness might have come about through the proportionally greater number of contacts of Zambian nurses with patients and the public than of foreigners; nurse violations of personal needs of patients for privacy and modesty might have come about because of overcrowding. Thus nurses were accused of 'talking too loudly' in preparing data sheets, allowing other patients to overhear. This was seen as embarrassing and potentially dangerous if unknown enemies overheard. They were accused of acting as if they were 'masters of the patients' in trying to discharge their responsibilities. They were the focus of arguments between the public and the hospital authorities.

Problems due to staff shortages were sometimes worsened by nurse attitudes, serving as an excuse for inactivity. The neglect of some patients was not simply imagined by the public. For example, I witnessed an old woman, the victim of a bar-room brawl, shivering with cold in a wheelchair for two hours waiting for the doctor, ignored by the nurses in attendance. A kind word, a sheet or blanket for cover, a basin of water to wash off caked blood and mud from her face and neck were not offered, despite pleas by the man who accompanied her. The nurses simply sat, waiting for the doctor.

Some antagonism in nurse-patient relations comes from cultural concepts of illness. The patient is not simply a victim of misfortune, but has a role in his victimisation by illness. The nurse judges the patient as either lacking in moral strength or in social support in his community, which is why he became ill. The very fact of illness is a sign of negative social-spiritual, as well as physical, manifestations. Hence the sick person is culturally evaluated and the medical problem becomes a subject of moral judgment. For example, female patients in obstetrics/gynaecology wards are the source of culturally-based negative emotional reactions. Women recovering from abortions are treated with prurient interest: I witnessed questions being asked about the private lives of these patients having nothing to do with medical aspects of their cases e.g. asking such women to name their lovers. If a lover is known by the Zambian medical staff, as often happens in the small world of subelite Lusaka, the patient will be the subject of gossip among the staff. In fact, many Zambian subelite women would not go to the hospital for abortions because staff members would tell their boyfriends who would then beat them. Women recovering from miscarriages are treated as morally deficient, since miscarriage is commonly believed to be a result of infidelity by the woman or her 'husband'. Nurses sometimes shout out, slap or ignore women having difficulties in childbirth because they too are suspected of moral frailty, since it is believed that such difficulties are the result of infidelity by the woman or the child's father.

Nurses are themselves sometimes ambivalent about their work. Among the nursing students, some said they would like to change occupations. While nurses and nursing students liked the idea of helping the sick, they disliked some of the work required of them. Aides were not always available to care for excreta of bedridden patients, a particular source of unease involving ritual contamination through contact with ritually polluting elements. Caring for strangers was distasteful; this and the fear of contact with those who had breached the moral order had to be overcome. Foreign supervisors' complaints about nurse irresponsibility derive from nurse difficulties in overcoming culturally-derived fears. Yet in overcoming many of their fears, hardening to the demands of their profession, they grow frustrated by their difficult role in the authoritarian chain of command. Some of the rudeness complained about by the public may derive from this frustration.

PROBLEMS WITH THE POSITION OF NURSES IN SOCIETY AT LARGE

Zambian nurses and student nurses are, along with similarly educated young women, a new stratum in society: the subelite. The subelite stratum originated in the first decade of independence, the product of expanding educational and training programmes that made possible employment in the modern sector. It is an incipient middle class, positioned between the elite (*apamwamba*) and the masses (*apansi*).

Zambian government policy on incomes contributes to the differentiation of subelite from other strata. As long as foreigners are recruited in certain occupational categories, working conditions and salary scales are roughly comparable to other countries. Local citizens are given similar conditions of service as foreigners to prevent social inequalities, particularly on a racial basis. By eliminating inequality between foreign and local employees in the same occupation, another form of inequality is created: that between the skilled occupational group and the mass of uneducated citizens. This division begins at the time of training. All education and training expenses are met by the government; trainees receive monthly stipends for personal expenses. Such is the case of nurses.

The new subelite status marks a radical change in the self-perceptions of young Zambian women. In the past, a woman's position in society was determined initially by that of her father and subsequently by that of her husband. Now the position of nurses and other young educated women is determined by their personal achievements, independent of their relationships to men. Student nurses are as conscious and proud of their achievement of mobility as are other young subelite women. Like other subelites, their perceptions of success are reinforced by society at large. Their stipends as students are greater than wages paid to unskilled male urban labourers supporting families. Nurses tend to spend their stipends almost exclusively on fashionable clothing, cosmetics and wigs, which are subelite status markers. Businessmen selling western style clothes regularly visit the student dormitories offering their wares, just as they visit other subelite urban residential neighbourhoods where unmarried women live. And just as married and unmarried elite and subelite men enjoy afterwork leisure hours visiting the flats of other young subelite women, so too the student nurse dormitories are popular 'cruising grounds'.

Thus the student nurses are desired as girlfriends, just as other young educated women, by men whose social position is higher than, or no less than equal to, their own. As such, nurses have the same advantages as other young subelite women: gifts of money, clothing, records, a gay life of dancing and drinking after a day of studies and hard work. They and the other young subelite women share the general feeling of being celebrated as the new kind of Zambian woman contributing to the development of her country, a type both desired and desirable. At the same time, the nurses are also subject to the same disadvantages of other subelite women in their private lives: the danger of refusing sexual advances, the broken promises of marriage, the conflicts with other women over the same man, the jealousy of boyfriends which I have described in detail elsewhere [Schuster, 1979b]. Student nurses face the same condemnation of their morality by the wider society that young subelite women in general face.

The premarital pregnancy rate, and therefore the drop out rate from nurse training programmes, was high: sometimes more than half. Unlike the smaller scale training programmes in other occupations, the sheer size of the nursing programme and the concentration of 100 or so young women in dormitories on hospital grounds, brought greater attention to the morality of these young women as an *occupational* group than was the case of other occupational groups among the subelite. Thus nurse dormitories are publicly referred to as brothels by leading members of the community. One account in the national daily newspaper, the *Times of Zambia* (11 November 1973) reports:

> In every city or town where there is a hospital or medical post, nurses are generally considered to be the most sexually liberated females.
>
> Most young men ... make fun about their weak morals. It is generally believed that a girl from a good home loses her moral values as soon as she enters the gates of a training school.
>
> Even if she tries to remain a hermit and lock herself in her room, the sound of cars which come to collect her friends, the gifts the owners of these cars bring, soon pull her out of her trenches into the open field ... It will take a long time before the general public can be made to believe that not every girl who joins the profession will become an educated prostitute. ...

Supervisors on the nurse training programmes privately lectured students on their morality and, together with Ministry of Health authorities, publicly defended them.[17] In an effort to cut down on pregnancy the birth control pill was quietly, if reluctantly, made available to the students who requested it, just as in other training programmes. In one hospital, a more determined effort was made to create discipline in the student dormitories by establishing a curfew and locking the building at night, a practice common in secondary boarding schools. The response of the students is indicative of their sense of their own high social status. Immediately following the imposition of the curfew and lock-up, a group went straight to the newspaper reporters who printed their complaint that they were being treated like 'maximum security prisoners'.[18] So loud was their protest that dormitories were reopened.

The perception by students of their social clout stems not only from their subelite status as financially independent, sexually desirable young urban women, but by their sense of security. Given the expansion of medical services, the serious shortage of registered nurses, the continued necessity, difficulty and expense of recruiting foreign nurses, and desire by the government to replace foreign with local personnel, there is every reason to feel self-confident. In stark contrast to the uneducated masses and even, more recently, other educated young people, nurses more than other subelites have no fear of unemployment. As long as they get their diplomas, the market belongs to them. The economy is not expanding at a sufficiently rapid rate to absorb all secondary school graduates, and the market for other subelite women's occupations is shrinking. For example, foreign typists are no longer recruited. But whereas economic development projects may expand slightly, remain stable or even falter, thereby affecting the job market, the government is morally committed to providing its population with health services. The more expensive and elaborate health service programmes may be cut back for lack of funds, but the training of nurses and their future employment security is assured.

SUMMARY AND CONCLUSIONS

Traditional Zambian society did not associate the healing process with young women. Modern health planners accepted without question the necessity of training young women as nurses to work in the modern health care setting. Recruits, who tended to be one generation removed from traditional life, imperfectly socialised into the modern health setting, tended to accept, unquestioningly, inherently conflicting traditional and western concepts of illness and healing, as did the wider society. Parallel conceptualisations and the overcrowding of medical facilities contributed to the growing perception of hospital settings as houses of death by the general public. Nurses, whose contact with the general public was greater than other health service personnel, came to be the focus of public abuse; their own ambivalence toward their work exacerbated this confrontation.

As actors in a wider society, nurses were part of the first generation of subelite urban women, sharing their problems as well as their pleasures. They were victims as well as beneficiaries of the gap between an egalitarian political ideology and the evolving socio-economic stratification system, and as such their position was fraught with ambivalence.

Their special problems as nurses resulted from the nature of their work. Illness is a time of vulnerability for both the sick person and his kin and friends. Society and the imperfectly socialised nurses were ambivalent about the sick person, who was seen as at least partially responsible for his condition. Ambivalence of attitude about the sick person as well as the role of the young Zambian woman as nurse (shared by both the nurse and the general public) combined with overcrowding to produce a hospital atmosphere characterised by tension, frustration, anger and disappointment. Yet such characteristics are also found in other institutions in the society. They are products of socio-cultural changes, often as painful as they are inevitable.

What of the future? One projection would be the following. The training of nurses will continue. With increased competition, standards of admission, and hence quality of trainees, will improve. With the passage of time society will accept the healing role of the young Zambian woman, and with the growing number of role models, adolescents will enter training with a clearer idea of the work involved. There will be mutual accommodation, adaptation, socialisation into appropriate roles among nurses, patients, and the visiting public. This view is accepted by some African medical practitioners trained in western medicine.

The view assumes a growing acceptance not only of modernisation with respect to the hospital setting but of westernisation, of the acceptance of western in lieu of traditional concepts of illness and healing. Yet the evidence is that many educated Africans continue to maintain dual conceptualisations, and that these remain, to date, unchallenged even in the training of health personnel. It also assumes the correctness of the western scientific model. Yet western medical technology has long erred in disregarding the health needs of the whole person, and has been highly inadequate in treating the health needs of all the citizens in developed western societies, in particular the poor. Health service training is therefore deeply inadequate in developed countries. It fails to incorporate notions of social harmony and the moral order of society as factors in illness; it is unaware of its own cultural biases in definitions of illness and health and the diagnosis and treatment of disease. Its mechanistic view of curing – witness the popular term 'medical management' – leaves little room for the role of self-will and social support, including the role of prayer. It often fails to encourage either consumer questioning of the practising physician or self criticism by members of the medical profession itself. African curative systems are in many ways more sensitive to the social and psychological functions of the healing process than are western curative systems. Dancing out a disease is, for example, sometimes an excellent remedy in psychoneurotic disorders. African systems cannot be dismissed totally as erroneous fantasies.

A great deal of serious work needs to be done on the role of the 'westernised' African nurse in healing African patients, and the insights that are gained from such research endeavours will substantially benefit the development of western medical practice. Such research has two problems to overcome. One is the continued cultural dependency on the west, since the west ignores what African nurses, in their close association with patients, understand about the condition of their charges. The second, related to the first, is also a product of cultural dependency. In the autocratic chain of command in African hospitals, the doctor remains as autocratic as he often is in the west. African nurses are no more able to challenge physicians than are western nurses in a traditional western hospital setting. African nurses must learn, as western nurses must also learn, to use their understanding of patients openly, to intellectualise their service and their contribution to the healing process. If African schools of nursing manage to overcome their cultural dependency on the west, they will truly contribute to the betterment of mankind.

NOTES

1. This raises an interesting issue. Historically, nursing in the west gained respectability when major responsibilities were removed from the female nurse and given to the male doctor. The western nurse is not permitted to make medical decisions and must defer to the authority of the doctor [*Corea, 1977:64–82*]. Western nurses today are agitating for the responsibilities that it is assumed non-western nurses must undertake.
2. As Corea points out [*1977:64 ff.*], the emphasis should be placed on 'lady'. Florence Nightingale's success was due in part to her aristocratic background and to her insistence that nurses were the handmaidens of doctors. In some ways the problem of nurses and nursing in Zambia is reminiscent of the problem in Great Britain in the last century.
3. Data on the problems of nurses and nursing were gathered in Lusaka, the capital city of Zambia, as part of a larger study of the adaptation to modern urban life of women of various educational, income and occupational categories in the decade following Zambia's independence from Great Britain. Research was conducted between January 1971 and August 1974 and again from September 1975 to August 1976. Formal interviews of 51 students enrolled in a three-year programme leading to a degree as Registered Nurse, and 16 practical nurses in a midwifery course were conducted in November 1973 at the University Teaching Hospital in Lusaka, using open-ended questionnaires, by three university student research assistants: Juliana Chileshe, Annie Mubanga, and Beatrice Mulamfu. Each interview was conducted in private, in the dormitory room of the interviewee, and took between one and two hours to complete. These were supplemented by informal observations of their life at work made during my visits to the hospital, as a patient, accompanying patients, and as a visitor to patients of various social statuses, during the course of anthropological fieldwork. In addition, over the period of fieldwork, newspaper clippings on nurses and on the problems of the Zambian health care service were collected. Fieldwork was supported by grants from the US National Institute of Mental Health and the University of Zambia. I wish to take this opportunity to thank my sponsors, research assistants and Benjamin Schuster who helped with data analysis.
4. For example, Helen Matanda and Liwito Siwale, Matrons at the University Teaching Hospital, trained at Chipembe, Mpilo and Scotland; Beatrice Shamoya, nurse and wife of the mayor of the Copperbelt town Ndola, trained at Chipembe, Mpilo and Salisbury [*Times of Zambia, 6 May 1972; and 11 March 1973*].
5. See: 'Fingers Crossed for More Nurses', [*Times of Zambia, 12 March 1972*]; 'Wanted, Urgently,' [*Times of Zambia, 16 April 1972*]; 'Swazi Nurses Shun Posts Here', [*Times of Zambia, 12 November 1972*].
6. In 1968, 284 women completed the course for enrolled nurses in private training programmes as against 80 in government programmes. However, there were no private programmes for State Registered nurses at the time. Twenty women completed government programmes in that year in state registered nursing [*Zambian Manpower: 62–3*].
7. The mean age of student nurses is twenty and of market women is twenty-four.
8. For an analysis of Lusaka's market women see [*Schuster, 1979a*].
9. Home areas for the other students were: 16 per cent each from North and South, 20 per cent from East, 2 per cent each for Copperbelt and Northwest, and 4 per cent each for Luapula and 'other'.
10. All the classic ethnographies of Zambia's ethnic groups mention this view of illness. See, for example, [*Colson, 1958:158–9*]; [*Gluckman, 1955:66, 223*]; [*Long, 1968:116*]; [*Richards, 1940:19*]; [*Turner, 1957:124, 126*]; [*Watson, 1958:152*].
11. See: ' "Useless" Nurses Shock', [*Times of Zambia, 24 March 1972*].
12. See: 'Where Nursing Comes Second to Social Action', [*Times of Zambia, 11 November 1973*]. Mazrui [1978] explores the common phenomenon of fear of watering down programmes in African higher educational institutions, particularly in East Africa.
13. See: 'The Problem of Our Rude Nurses', [*Zambia Daily Mail, 26 April 1976*]; 'Union Raps Hospital Matrons', [*Times of Zambia, 25 August 1971*]; 'Zulu Lashes at "Inhuman" Ndola Hospital Staff', [*Zambia Daily Mail, 19 January 1973*]; 'Kankasa Hits out at Nurses' Lack of Devotion', [*Times of Zambia, 9 March 1973*]; 'The Mail Man, and the Angry Nurse', [*Zambia Daily Mail, 20 July 1972*]; see also, *Zambia Daily Mail* editorials, [*11 September 1971*]; [*29 December 1971*]; *Times of Zambia* editorial, [*11 September 1971*].
14. See: 'Bouquet for Nurses', [*Zambia Daily Mail, 30 July 1971*].
15. The same is found in South Africa [*Kuper, 1965*].

16. See: 'Bouquet for Nurses' [op. cit.].
17. See: 'Ministry Stands by Nurses', [*Times of Zambia, 30 December 1972*].
18. See: 'It's Like a Prison', [*Times of Zambia, 4 April 1972*].

REFERENCES

Asuni, Tolani, 1979, 'The Dilemma of Traditional Healing with Special Reference to Nigeria' in *Social Science and Medicine*, Vol. 13B, 33–9.
Boserup, Ester, 1970, *Woman's Role in Economic Development*, New York: St. Martin's Press, Inc.
Bossert, Thomas, 1979a, 'Health and Health Care in Latin America' in *Latin American Research Review*, Vol. XIV, 247–51.
Bossert, Thomas, 1979b, 'Health Problems in Africa and Latin America: Adopting the Primary Care Approach', in *Social Science and Medicine*, Vol. 13C, 65–8.
Brink, Pamela, 1979, 'Medical Anthropologists in Schools of Nursing', in *Medical Anthropology*, Vol. 3, 297–307.
Bryant, John, 1969, *Health and the Developing World*, Ithaca: Cornell University Press.
Colson, Elizabeth, 1958, *Marriage and Family Among the Plateau Tonga of Northern Rhodesia*, Manchester: Manchester University Press.
Corea, Gina, 1977, *The Hidden Malpractice*, New York: Jove Publications Inc. (Harcourt Brace Jovanovich).
Department of State, United States Agency for International Development, Office of Women in Development, 1978, *Report on Women in Development*, Washington, D.C.
Frankenberg, Ronald, 1969, 'Man, Society and Health: Towards the Definition of the Role of Sociology in the Development of Zambian Medicine', in *African Social Research*, Vol. VIII, 573–8.
Gish, Oscar, 1979, 'The Political Economy of Primary Care and Health by the People: An Historical Explanation', in *Issue*, Vol. IX, 6–13.
Gluckman, Max, 1955, *The Judicial Process among the Barotse of Northern Rhodesia*, Manchester: Manchester University Press.
Government of the Republic of Zambia, Government Printing Office, Lusaka, 1970, *Statistical Year Book*; 1971, *Statistical Year Book*; 1971, *Second National Development Plan*; 1971, *Zambian Manpower*; 1969, *Survey of Occupations in 1969*.
Herskovitz, Melville, 1962, *The Human Factor in Changing Africa*, New York: Vintage Books (Random House).
Imperato, Pascal, 1979, 'Interface of Traditional and Modern Medicine in Mali', in *Issue*, Vol. IX, 14–18.
Joseph, Stephen, 1979, 'Innovation and Constraints in Health Manpower Policy: A Case History of Medical Education Development in Cameroun', in *Social Science and Medicine*, Vol. 13B, 137–42.
King, Maurice (ed.), 1966, *Medical Care in Developing Countries*, Nairobi: Oxford University Press.
Kleinman, Arthur, 1978, 'International Health Care Planning from an Ethnomedical Perspective: Critique and Recommendations for Change', in *Medical Anthropology*, Vol. 2, 71–93.
Kuper, Hilda, 1965, 'Nurses', in *An African Bourgeoisie*, Leo Kuper, New Haven: Yale University Press.
Long, Norman, 1968, *Social Change and the Individual*, Manchester: Manchester University Press.
Mazrui, Ali, 1978, *Political Values and the Educated Class in Africa*, London: Heinemann.
Mburu, F. M., 1979, 'Rhetoric-Implementation Gap in Health Policy and Health Services Delivery for a Rural Population in a Developing Country', in *Social Science and Medicine*, Vol. 13A, 577–83.
Meebelo, Henry, 1973, *Main Currents of Zambian Humanist Thought*, Lusaka: Oxford University Press.
Mwanakatwe, J. M., 1968, *The Growth of Education in Zambia Since Independence*, Lusaka: Oxford University Press.
Nelson, Nici, 1979, *Why has Development Neglected Rural Women?* Oxford: Pergamon Press.
Richards, Audrey, 1940, *Bemba Marriage and Modern Economic Conditions*, Rhodes-Livingstone Paper, No. 3.
Schuster, Ilsa, 1979a, 'Marginal Lives: Conflict and Contradiction in the Position of Female Traders in

Lusaka, Zambia'. Paper presented at the Symposium, 'Women and Work in Africa', University of Illinois at Urbana-Champaign, 29 April–1 May 1979.

Schuster, Ilsa, 1979b, *New Women of Lusaka*, Palo Alto: Mayfield Publishing Company.

Seidman, Ann, 1974, 'The Distorted Growth of Import-Substitution Industry; the Zambian Case', in *The Journal of Modern African Studies*, Vol. XII, 601–31.

Taylor, Carl, 1979, 'Implications for the Delivery of Health Care', in *Social Science and Medicine*, Vol. 13B, 77–84.

Times of Zambia, 25 August 1971; 11 September 1971; 12 March 1972; 24 March 1972; 4 April 1972; 16 April 1972; 6 May 1972; 12 November 1972; 30 December 1972; 9 March 1973; 11 March 1973; 11 November 1973.

Turner, Victor, 1957, *Schism and Continuity in an African Society*, Manchester: Manchester University Press.

Turner, Victor, 1964, 'An Ndembu Doctor in Practice', in *Magic, Faith and Healing*, Ari Kiev (ed.), Glencoe: Free Press, 230–63.

Watson, W., 1958, *Tribal Cohesion in a Money Economy*, Manchester: Manchester University Press.

Zambia Daily Mail, 30 July 1971; 11 September 1971; 20 July 1972; 19 January 1973; 26 April 1976.

Development Policies in Tanzania – Some Implications for Women

by Pat Caplan

Recent development policies in Tanzania, notably in the areas of land-holding, re-settlement of villages, and housing, may well have important implications for women. Under the traditional system, women enjoyed a relatively large degree of autonomy, particularly because of their rights to hold land as individuals, rather than through their husbands. Because many policies are based on the assumption that productive and consumption units are households headed by males, and because of the construction of a new form of 'family', there is a possibility that women will be re-defined as dependents and thus lose much of their autonomy.

Government development policies which have recently been implemented in Tanzania have begun to affect village life on the coast, the area with which this article is concerned. As yet, changes are not very great, but they are likely to accelerate, and in particular, to have important implications for women. Three policies will be considered.

The first policy considered in this article concerns rights to land, both cultivable and residential. Soon after independence, it was declared that all land belonged to the nation, and that any citizen could take up and cultivate a piece of unused land. The intention of policy, as was made clear in the Arusha Declaration,[1] was to prevent the growth of a class of speculators and absentee landlords. However, in areas such as Tanzania where most cultivation is on a shifting basis, and where rights are allocated on the basis of descent, the new laws have raised certain problems.

Secondly, in the mid-seventies, Tanzania instituted a 'villagisation' policy, by which people were moved into nucleated villages. This policy was devised to fit the needs of the majority of inhabitants of inland Tanzania, who previously lived spread out in tiny hamlets, thus making it virtually impossible to organise services such as schooling, medical care and water supplies. On the coast, however, nucleated villages have been the pattern for a long time, but nonetheless, people in outlying areas were moved into the centre of villages, and even some of those already living in the centre were allocated new house sites.

The third policy, which was initiated in this area in 1976, was a 'better housing' (*nyumba bora*) campaign, an attempt to persuade people to try and build more durable houses with corrugated iron roofs, and cement floors, rather than the houses and huts made of local materials such as palm leaves, mud and mangrove poles.

THE AREA AND ITS ECONOMY

The area in which field-work[2] was carried out between 1965 and 1967 and again in 1976, is the north part of Mafia Island,[3] which lies some 80 miles to the south of Dar es Salaam. The north of the island, like many other parts of the coast, has nucleated villages, each surrounded by a belt of bush land cultivated on a shifting pattern. The people grow rice, millet, sweet potatoes, corn, cassava, and various vegetables. All of these crops are for their own subsistence. In the mid 1960s, most households produced enough for around nine months of the year, but by 1976, with the intensification of cassava cultivation, there was a greater degree of self-sufficiency. Villagers also cultivate coconut palms, and sell the copra for cash. Palms are individually owned, may be bought and sold, and are inherited according to Islamic law, by which all children receive a share, except that women only receive half a man's portion. The money from the sale of copra is used to buy clothes, pay taxes, and for items of food not produced locally, such as tea and sugar.

In addition to cultivation, there is a considerable amount of fishing, although no one is a full-time specialist. Some men fish only for their household's consumption, others sell any extra within the village, while a minority fishes more intensively, using traps and large nets, and takes the catch, after it has been dried or smoked, for sale to Dar es Salaam.

Economic differentiation is not highly developed in this area, because everyone is dependent upon cultivation. However, some people own more coconut trees than others, and in general, men own twice as many trees as women. Usually, too, older people own more trees than younger ones who have not yet inherited from their parents. Other methods by which men earn cash are by migration to Dar es Salaam for short periods, by trading in goods from Mafia to Dar (exporting dried fish and mats and importing clothes and other small personal items), and by keeping cattle and selling milk, or, occasionally a beast for slaughter on a ritual occasion. Women earn cash by cutting grass (ukindu), drying it, and then either selling it in its raw state, or else plaiting long coloured strips which are sewn into mats for which the island is famous.

Thus although cash is not insignificant, land remains the most important factor of production. The system of land tenure described below ensured a highly egalitarian distribution of this major resource.

Cultivation Rights

(a) bush land. The bush land in northern Mafia lies on a ridge which forms a back-bone to this part of the island. Here the soil is clay, whereas around the villages, which are at sea level, it is sandy, and more suitable for coconut cultivation. The soil on the ridge is thin, and can only be cultivated for a year at a time, after which it is left for at least six years before being used again. The techniques of cultivation are for the men to cut down the trees and bushes which have grown up since the last time, leave them to dry out, and then set fire to the area. The resulting cleared patches of land are then planted up by the women.

Although each married couple or single person cultivates their own field, some of the work is done collectively. For example, the men fire the bush together, and they then build one single fence to keep out pests from a number of fields. Women often exchange labour in each other's fields, and some of them form groups to cook collectively during the agricultural season. Until the mid 1960s, people only obtained bush land through membership of one or other of the cognatic descent groups which controlled an area. Because most people belong to more than one descent group (since they inherit the membership of both their father's and mother's groups), they usually have plenty of choice about where to cultivate.

In 1966, in the village in which I was working, the first case arose of a man who went and cleared a piece of bush land which belonged to a group of which he was not a member. When the elders of that group took him before the Village Development Committee (VDC) it was soon realised that the case was problematic. They referred it to the District Court, where the man claimed that he was merely exercising his rights as a citizen, and was given permission to continue his cultivation.

By 1976, however, very few people had availed themselves of such rights. Most continued to obtain land through their descent groups. For the majority of cases, it simply would not have been worthwhile to risk the bad feelings (and possible withdrawal of cooperation) caused by flouting the established customs. There is plenty of bush land, and those who do not have access to the area they want can usually get some in another area, or can 'beg' from someone who does have a right, using ties of affinity or friendship.

Two possible developments may, however, cause the old system to change more rapidly. One is a new cultivation technique. In one northern village, a large area of land was cleared, and it was proposed to plough it, initially using oxen (which however soon died), and then a tractor. Such an innovation, if it were to be successful, would require such inputs as fertiliser for the land to continue to yield crops for a long enough period to make the large expenditure of labour and money incurred by hiring the tractor worthwhile. If such a development became widespread, then obviously the cognatic descent groups would lose their main function, and would probably cease to exist. The other possible factor is the increase in population. In 1967, I calculated that, given the current population and the agricultural techniques then in use, there was sufficient land, indeed perhaps some to spare. But the population of this area appears to be growing very rapidly (unfortunately I was not able to carry out a census in 1976, but my impressions are backed up by the official census figures for Mafia Island). Once land becomes scarce, then rights to it are likely to be more sharply defined, and those people who have rights less willing to let others use them.

(b) meadow land. In addition to the bush land, there is a certain amount of meadow land lying within the village boundaries which is flooded during the wet season. This land produces a more prolific crop of rice, and, if it is manured by tethering cattle on it, can also produce a second crop of sweet potatoes. It can thus be cultivated on a semi-permanent basis. Rights to most of this meadow land are obtained through ownership of the coconut trees which border it, and it is thus held on an individual basis, and inherited as part of an estate. It is striking that much of this land is owned by women, who try to ensure that in the distribution of their parents' trees, some of those bordering meadow land go to them. The reason for this is that in the case of divorce, which is very frequent on the coast, a woman can easily cultivate a meadow field on her own; it requires no bush to be cut down. Some women, even when they are married, continue to cultivate a meadow field as well as a bush field. Meadow land does not appear to have been affected by recent changes in land laws.

(c) cassava fields. Soon after independence, the agricultural office on Mafia began a vigorous campaign to intensify cassava cultivation. In each of the northern villages, areas were set aside for it, and anyone could go and use some of this land. Previously, such land had been part of the areas controlled by the descent groups, but this was no longer the case. The move aroused little opposition, and more and more men began to cultivate this hardy and relatively easy-to-grow crop. By 1976, most men in the village had a cassava field, which meant that they worked somewhat harder than before. Women rarely plant or grow cassava, although they may occasionally help to weed their husbands' fields. On the whole, they have more than enough to do with the cultivation of the bush or meadow fields. The cassava grown by the men is primarily for household consumption.

Houses and House Sites

On most parts of the coast, a person can build a house if he or she owns coconut trees in that area; otherwise, the permission of the owner must be sought. Since most people own trees in various parts of the village, there is usually a fairly wide choice of site for residence, and during an adult's life-time, he or she may move a number of times. For instance, a fisherman will try to be as close to the sea as possible; an older person to be near the centre of the village, a religious person near to a mosque and so on. Quite a number of villagers own trees in villages other than the one where they reside, as well as possibly having rights to bush land there through membership of a descent group. It is perfectly possible for such people to build a house and move there, and this happens not infrequently.

Houses on the coast of Tanzania are of three main types. Wealthy people live in houses built of stone or coral rag, which can be plastered and whitewashed (*nyumba safi*); some such houses have several floors. They are more typical of urban, rather than rural areas, although in some rural areas, which have long had a plantation economy and great economic differentiation (for instance in southern Mafia), such houses are found. There are no stone houses in northern Mafia.

The second type of house (*nyumba*), and probably the most common, is built of a framework of mangrove poles, with small branches interlaced to form a wattle, and the whole filled in with mud. The roof is of thatch made from coconut palm fronds (*makuti*). Such houses, which are always single-storey, consist of one or more rooms, an open verandah at the front, and a fenced-off courtyard containing a separate kitchen and bathroom to the rear. Houses of this type, if kept in good repair, can easily last a generation.

The third type is the simplest form of housing, known as a hut (*kibanda*), which has only a minimal wooden framework, and both walls and roof made of coconut palm fronds. Such structures can be very quickly erected, and can last for a few years if the roof is maintained.

The labour involved in building the houses in northern Mafia is primarily drawn from the household. Men cut the mangrove poles, and cut down palm fronds. Women collect the mud and fill in the walls. Some people do get their kin to help them; others may pay a casual labourer, but it is rare to find large amounts of cash being expended on a house, nor are the services of specialists required.

In this area, the difference between people who reside in a house (*nyumba*) and those who live in a hut (*kibanda*) is only partly connected with economic status; more important is their stage in the life cycle, and in the developmental cycle of the household, which is examined below.

Houses, then, are built primarily of local materials, by non-specialists, and they do not have any cash value – they are neither sold nor rented, and they do not count as a capital asset in the division of a deceased person's estate.

THE HOUSEHOLD AND ITS DEVELOPMENTAL CYCLE

In this area of northern Mafia, and on other parts of the coast with a similar economy, the household consists primarily of a group of people who eat together. In the majority of cases, households consist of a nuclear family occupying a house, but there is a substantial minority of cases which do not conform to this pattern. For instance, a divorced woman moves into her own hut, and sets up a separate household by cooking for herself and her children. A teenage boy moves out of his parents' house and builds a hut alongside it, but he still continues to eat with the family, and thus forms part of the household.

A household is not a sharply defined production and consumption unit in all respects. In many important ways, production units are both larger and smaller than the household. Mention has already been made of collective labour, which involves a number of households. Even more important is the fact that although household members may cooperate in cultivation, they have separate and individual rights to the products of that labour.

As already stated, some married couples choose to cultivate separately. In the majority of cases, they cultivate a joint field, plus a cassava field for the husband, and a rice/sweet potato meadow field for the wife. As soon as boys and girls reach their early teens, and before they are married, they begin cultivating their own small fields. In all cases where a person cultivates a field alone, the produce belongs to him or her. In the case of joint cultivation, there are joint rights. Some couples for example split the crop after harvest, and store it separately. Under Islamic law,[4] a husband is responsible for providing his wife and children with food and clothes. Technically, then, a wife can do what she likes with her share of the harvest, although most contribute it to the food eaten by the household. However, women, like men, contribute as individuals to the rituals of kin, and a woman can thus feel that a generous contribution from her is a gift from her own property, not a drain on household resources. To a large extent, then, the household is a collection of autonomous individuals; each owns his or her own property, in the form of coconut trees, land rights, and the produce of labour. There is a certain amount of cooperation between household members, and the rights to separate the joint property may not be exercised, for instance the harvest may not be divided; nonetheless, such rights remain, and can be activated at any time, particularly in the event of a divorce, when everything must be divided equally.

There are also strongly developed notions of privacy in this society. One of the ways in which this manifests itself, is that no two adults, other than a married couple, will share the same house. Under certain circumstances, they may form a household, in that the inhabitants of more than one house eat together (e.g. a married couple and their adult but as yet unmarried son). However, all adults have a house of their own, even if that is a hut, rather than a proper house. The three categories of people who in the course of a life-time are likely to live in huts, are youths, old people, and divorced women. Each of these are now considered in turn.

The Flexibility of Temporary Housing

(a) teenage boys. When they reach puberty, boys move into their own huts alongside their parents' house. They sleep there at night, and entertain their (male) friends, but continue to eat from the parental kitchen. The reason for this custom is the growing 'shame' said to be felt by a boy as he becomes cognisant of his parents' sexual activities. It also helps to alleviate the tension often felt between parents and children at this stage of life. In other words, the privacy of both parties is respected. Later, when a young boy gets married, he and his wife build a proper house of their own, which may or may not be near to his parents' house.

Young girls do not have the same privilege, and indeed, once they reach puberty, are more confined to the house than before, for virginity on marriage is considered important. Until recently, many of them were completely secluded from first menstruation to marriage, a period which might last a year or two. At the time of my re-visit in 1976, this was a rare practice, and all the girls in their early teens were in school. Girls, unlike boys, are only considered to be social adults on marriage, which is why it is possible for them to go on sharing a house with their parents.

(b) old people. In this area, the norm is for old people to continue cultivating for as long as possible, and they also continue to live in their own houses, even if they no longer have any children living with them. Frequently, one or more grandchildren will be sent to live with grandparents in the widespread practice known as '*ulezi*' – up-bringing or fostering. In one village, in 1966, a quarter of the children were living with people other than their parents, most of them with grandparents, sometimes with childless aunts and uncles. It is thus very rare for an old person to live completely alone.

Women and men over fifty-five whose spouse dies or divorces them are unlikely to re-marry. If alone, such a person is likely to move near to the house of a son or daughter, and build a hut there. Most women will continue to cook for themselves for as long as possible, whereas elderly men, and incapacitated women, will have to receive food from the main kitchen. The need for privacy and independence is strongly stressed. One friend of mine, a woman in her late thirties, was living in a small hut after her divorce, next to her widowed mother in another hut alongside. These women shared cooking, but stated 'We each need our own house, so that we don't get in each other's way, especially when friends come visiting'.

The following statement by a woman in her early forties about her own elderly widowed mother makes these points even more forcibly:

> My mother is looked after by her children, myself, my sister, and my three brothers. She depends on us now, she has no strength left. She can't cultivate. So we women take our hoes and do it for her. And the men take

their bill-hooks and go and cut down some bush. Then we go and plant. We do all this for her because she is our parent, and her strength is finished. Anyone who fells green coconuts takes one to her. Anyone who buys a kilo or two of flour gives some to mother. And if any of the men get fish, mother should be given some. When they fell ripe coconuts, she should also be given one (for cooking). So that we can say that if an old person's strength is finished, then he or she depends on the children, and the children are people like us.

Old people live near to their children – where else would they go? Now she has become like a child, and we are like her parents, because we have to look for food to give her, since she hasn't any means of doing so herself. So we look after her until her strength is finished, and her days are ended, and God takes her and that's the end.

Of course, old people continue to work and to cultivate for as long as possible. For instance, they might plait grass and sew the strips together to make mats to sell to get some money to buy food and clothes. But if her strength is finished, then she becomes like a small child, and is looked after by her children. You have to cook for her, fetch water, wash her clothes, and do everything.

However, such an old person will still have her own house, except that if she gets sick (or a man if your parent is your father) then you take that person into your house to nurse them until he or she is well again, and can go back to their own house.

What is striking about this statement is the extent to which the independence of the old person is preserved for as long as possible. He or she has a field, even if most of the cultivation is done by the children. Furthermore, they will have their own house, even when no longer capable of cooking or looking after themselves.

(c) divorced women. There is a high rate of divorce on the East African coast. A man can divorce his wife by pronouncing the formula three times. For a woman it is more problematic. She can try to persuade her husband to give her a divorce, by making life as unpleasant as possible for him, but if he proves recalcitrant, she may have to go to the District Court in the south of the island. She is frequently able to obtain a divorce there on the grounds of 'inadequate maintenance' – for example, her husband hasn't bought her any new clothes – and given the relative poverty of most villagers, this is not difficult to substantiate.

When a husband divorces his wife, he is supposed to take her back to her parents, and divorced women most commonly live near to a parent, at least for a while. If they are below the age of menopause, they are likely to re-marry. However, some women stay alone for long periods, and they are able to manage by themselves largely because of their land rights. They can usually persuade a male relative to 'cut' a bush field for them, if that is where they want to cultivate; otherwise they can gain access to meadow land, which is the more usual course of action. Meadow land, as previously stated, does not need any male labour input, except some fencing, and since the land can be cultivated for several years at a time, this does not need to be done every year.

Some women move out to live on their meadow land, and build a hut there, with the help of their male kin, as in the following case of a divorced woman of around forty years who explained:

> This house was built for me by my cousin, my mother's brother's son. And the fence around the field by various youngsters – when I see them passing I ask them to do a bit for me. I grow sweet potatoes here, and rice and bananas. I can manage all the work on my own. As for cash expenses, I plait grass and sew mats and sell them, or I cut and dry grass for sale. I have a few coconut trees, so I get the nuts felled and I sell them too. My three (grown-up) sons are in Dar es Salaam working; they only come home on leave, or sometimes I visit them there. I have three brothers living in Zanzibar, and a brother here in the village, together with an older sister. My father is here with me, he isn't too well these days, so I have to look after him. My older brother helps me sometimes, either by fishing, or by assisting in cultivation.

Such a woman can manage on her own for the following reasons: (i) she has her own land rights, (ii) she can do most of the work on her own, (iii) she can get cash from the sale of copra and mats, (iv) because the help she needs from male kin is minimal – mainly building a hut and fencing her field – such help is very rarely refused. A divorced woman is not a burden to her kin, and they are thus unlikely to try and force her to go back to her husband.

A second case study of a divorced woman who chose to leave her husband makes the point even more clearly: Mwajuma is a woman in her early forties who after a first brief unhappy marriage, married Mohammed and had ten children by him over a twenty-year period. Nonetheless, the marriage was a stormy one and Mohammed's infidelities were notorious. In 1976, Mwajuma decided that she had had enough and she left her husband. She explained her situation thus:

> My husband and I have separated, as you know. We just can't communicate any more. I haven't yet got my formal divorce [since Mohammed wanted her to go back], but even when I do get it, I shall still have the children to look after. Men don't bring up children on their own – they are always on the move. That husband of mine might not be home for two days together, so do you think I'll let him bring up the children? No, I must be the one to bring them up, although he must help me by contributing to their maintenance.
>
> As for me, I'll go and find any place in which I can build a little hut. I shall move there. I don't have to stay here at my natal home. I can cut palm leaves and dry them to get money, and look for clay and make pots, and plait strips and make mats too – whatever is available at the time. I've got a few coconuts which I inherited from my deceased father, some here where I'm living now next to my mother, and some on the outskirts of the village, where I plan to go and live myself. We'll have to divide this year's harvest half and half. But as for the house, he can have it, what good it is to me?

Women, then, do have a certain amount of autonomy in their lives. They can leave their husbands and manage to feed themselves and their children, albeit with greater difficulty than when living with a husband, because of men's greater access to cash. They can earn money from their own coconut trees and from making mats. They can obtain land. They have residential rights on their own account, and can usually get help in building a hut.

As part of the villagisation campaign described at the beginning of this paper, many people were asked to move their house sites. In the village studied most intensively, a whole hamlet on the southern outskirts of the village was moved into the main area. House sites were allocated on a random basis, and not according to whether or not people owned coconut trees. The idea was that each house should have an acre of kitchen garden around it, but people asked how they were to find time to cultivate this, in addition to rice and cassava fields. Naturally, many of them resented having to abandon their existing houses, and all complained that the rules about residential rights being conferred by ownership of coconut trees were being ignored.[5]

Soon after the villagisation policy had been implemented, the 'better housing' campaign began. A district official addressed a meeting of all the men in the village thus:

> Let there be one house, and let that house be built according to the family that you have. Because there are some people who are very old or blind, and they can't look after themselves, so if you give them a place of their own, it's a waste of time, for that old person needs taking care of. So if that is the situation you must build a house which is sufficient for you, for your wife, for the old man or woman, and that house should be big enough for all of you. But to build one small hut here, and another over there in a corner, that is not a good way to lay out a village. If you don't want to see the old people all the time, then give them their door and you have yours on the other side, so that you don't keep on meeting each other. No more of this business of building little huts in corners for youths, for it is not like a village, but a runaways' camp. We want everyone to have proper houses (*nyumba safi*). So try and build with at least three rooms, try to get corrugated iron for the roof, and cement floors. If you can't manage all at once, buy a little at a time. We don't want people living any more in houses which are full of snakes and mice.

There are several points in this speech which need further examination. First of all, there is concern that many of the houses in the village are of poor quality, e.g. they harbour 'snakes and mice'. Furthermore, the way in which houses are laid out, and the fact that some are huts rather than houses, is not thought to be 'good planning'.[6] Indeed, the official went on to say that houses should be laid out in straight lines. Secondly, there is little acknowledgement of the need for privacy which is an important concept in this society. Nor is the extreme flexibility of the current residential patterns perceived. Houses can be built to suit the needs of one or more people – they can be built fairly easily, and because there is relatively little capital investment in them, ownership does not become an important issue. Once houses are built of imported materials, for cash, and using specialist labour, then they become capital assets. What is to happen when a couple divorces? How will young people acquire a house? What will be the effect on proximate generations of parents living under the same roof as their teenage sons, or their elderly parents? Or on divorced women who cannot obtain a house of their own, but must move in with kin?

There was reference in the speech to the men as 'You and your families'. In Swahili, the term 'family', in the sense of a bounded domestic group does not exist, as I have already shown in the discussion of the household. Indeed, it has been necessary to take the English term and turn it into a Swahili form *'familia'*. Such a linguistic usage contains a number of premises – that the unit in society is 'a man and *his* family', and that this unit requires a house and an area of land. In other words, concepts foreign to this society, of closely bounded units in the form of households, possessing property in the form of a house and land, and headed by a male, are being introduced. If this becomes a reality, then women, along with old people, will have lost much of their autonomy.

This particular speech which I have analysed, is by no means an isolated instance. Much of the planning in Tanzania seems to be based on this assumption. For instance, people who were moved into *ujamaa* (collective) villages were allocated land and housing in family units, and in some areas, at least initially, the women found themselves considerably worse off under the new system.[7] What is not always realised by planners and officials is just how many rights, and how much autonomy women possessed in many parts of the country under the traditional system, and in particular, that they held land in their own right and not as the dependent of a male. This applied particularly to the matrilineal areas of the country, and also to the coast. This is something difficult for city-bred people, used to the idea of a male wage-earner and a dependent wife and children to understand.[8]

CONCLUSION

This article does not seek to suggest that the status quo should be preserved; development in the rural areas must take place, agricultural techniques and productivity must be improved if the mass of Tanzanians are to see a rise in their standard of living. Even in an area such as the one described in this article, women have always had a harder life than men, carrying a much greater burden of work. There is a widespread realisation of this at all levels in Tanzania. But in planning for greater equality, between town and country, and women and men, it is surely important to preserve the best in the old system, as well as introducing the new.[9] This means ensuring the autonomy of individuals, rather than their dependence, in order that they may together work to make socialism a reality, which means, among other things, constructing a society in which patriarchy, ageism and sexism have no place.

NOTES

1. Cf [*Nyerere 1968: 231–56*].
2. Field-work between 1965 and 1967 was financed by a University of London Postgraduate Scholarship, and a scholarship from the Worshipful Company of Goldsmiths. My re-visit in 1976 was for the purposes of making a film for the BBC.
3. For further information on this area, cf Caplan [*1969*], [*1975*], [*1976*], [*1978*], [*1981*].

4. Cf [*El-Busaidy 1962:19*].
5. From two recent articles on 'Operation Sogeza' [*Mwapachu, and De Vries and Fortmann*, both *1979*], it seems likely that the experience in northern Mafia was by no means unusual.
6. Similarly, De Vries and Fortmann comment that bureaucrats insisted on houses being built in straight lines, and that some people had to move just 50 feet to comply with this! [*Ibid:135*].
7. A trenchant criticism of the early *ujamaa* villages from this viewpoint appears in Brain [*1975*].
8. Yet this notion is very specific to a particular mode of production, namely capitalism, as much recent marxist and feminist analysis has shown. Cf Land [*1980*] for a discussion of the way in which the state and capitalism together have structured 'the family' in Britain.
9. In this respect, Engels' [*1891*] discussion of the emergence of 'the family' from the wider clan and kinship organisation, its connection with the resultant oppression of women, remains instructive.

REFERENCES

Al Busaidy, Hamed Bin Saleh, 1962, *Ndoa na Talaka*, Nairobi: East African Literature Bureau.
Brain, James, 1975, 'The Position of Women on Rural Development Schemes in Tanzania', *Ufahamu*, VI, 1, Los Angeles.
Caplan, A. P., 1975, *Choice and Constraint in a Swahili Community*, London: International African Institute/OUP.
—, 1976, 'Boys' circumcision and girls' puberty rites on Mafia Island, Tanzania', *Africa*, Vol. 46, No. 1., London.
—, 1978, 'The Swahili of Chole Island, Tanzania' in *Face Values*, ed. A. Sutherland, BBC/RAI.
—, 1981 (in press), 'Gender, Ideology and Modes of Production on the East African Coast' in *Pwani: Essays to James Kirkman*, ed. J. de Vere Allen.
De Vries, J., and Fortmann, L., 1979, 'Large-scale villagization: Operation Sogeza in Iringa Region', in *African Socialism in Practice*, ed. A. Coulson, Nottingham, England: Spokesman Press.
Engels, F., 1972, *The Origins of the Family, Private Property and the State*, New York: International (originally published 1891).
Land, H., 1980, 'The Family Wage', *Feminist Review*, 6, London.
Mwapachu, J. V., 1979, 'Operation Planned Villages in Rural Tanzania' in *African Socialism in Practice*, ed. A. Coulson, Nottingham, England: Spokesman Press.
Nyerere, J., and the National Executive of TANU, 1968, 'The Arusha Declaration' (of 1967) in Nyerere, J., *Freedom and Socialism*, London: OUP.

Gambian Women: Unequal Partners in Rice Development Projects?

Jennie Dey*

Agricultural development projects usually channel inputs to male household heads on the assumption that they control the land, labour, crops and finances. This assumption is challenged for the Mandinka: women cultivate rainfed rice, having ownership or use-rights to rice land, while men control upland and grow groundnuts and millets. Both cultivate household and personal crops. Three development projects introduced irrigated rice to men who therefore control this land and crop. Failure to involve women in rice development schemes has not only increased their economic dependence on men but is also a major reason for deficiencies in these projects and low national rice production.

I. INTRODUCTION

A number of studies have drawn attention to a sexual division of labour in Third World agriculture, where men and women are either responsible for separate field operations or they cultivate different crops. While recognising this, few have gone on to explore the corollary: that there may be a parallel division in the control of the crops. As a result, most agricultural development projects have been based on an implicit assumption that, regardless of how labour is organised, all cultivation is carried out on behalf of the 'household' unit, and that the land, labour, crops and finances are under the control of the 'household' head. The latter is usually the only direct participant in agricultural development projects, as planners assume that other household members will automatically take part and that any increased income accruing to the head will also benefit them.

Three development projects which introduced dry and rainy season irrigated rice to farmers in The Gambia, a country in which cultivation had, until 1966, been confined to the rainy season, show that this assumption was unfounded in the case of The Gambia. Moreover, failure to appreciate the division of labour and variations in the control of different crops has not only led to deficiencies in project design but has also increased the divisions in the household with women gaining far less than men. This paper explores these issues within the context of the existing farming system of the Mandinka, the predominant ethnic group in The Gambia.

---

* Jennie Dey is currently taking part in an Overseas Development Administration team drawing up a national food supply strategy for The Gambia. This paper is based on research carried out in the Mandinka village of Saruja, MacCarthy Island Division, between March 1977–November 1978, with two visits of three weeks each in March 1976 and March 1980.

II. POSITION OF WOMEN WITHIN THE FARMING SYSTEM

The position of women within the Mandinka farming system can only be analysed in comparison with the relative position of men. Both can be understood in terms of reciprocal rights and duties which are complementary, fairly balanced, and sanctioned by custom. These are outlined in more detail below and cover the division of labour; differences between food and cash crops; the organisation of labour; the control of crops and revenues; and the ownership and control of land.

(i) Sexual Division of Labour

Francis Moore, a factor working on the River Gambia in the early eighteenth century, first drew attention to what was clearly a well-established division of labour between men and women. He observed [*Moore, 1738:127*] that 'The Men work the Corn Ground, and the Women and Girls the Rice Ground'.

This division of labour reflects differences in land types and crops. Women have been traditionally responsible for growing rice in tidal swamps, inland depressions and on hydromorphic soils while men have cultivated the free-draining upland. Their crops were primarily sorghum and millet, to which maize was added on its introduction from the Americas in the sixteenth century. Groundnuts, introduced from the Americas in the eighteenth century, are grown in rotation or inter-cropped with sorghum and millet. After 1830 groundnut production expanded rapidly and by the end of the century groundnuts had become the major cash crop of the region. They are grown largely by men,[1] often at the expense of their sorghum and millet, while women continue to grow the subsistence rice crop.

(ii) Crops for Auto-Consumption or Cash

There is an important distinction between *maruo* crops that are for consumption by the household and the *kamanyango* crops that belong to the cultivator and may be disposed of as he or she wishes. The *maruo* crop should not, in principle, be sold although small quantities are sold or exchanged for other basic items of food. Men cultivate sorghum, millet, maize and some groundnuts while women grow rice as *maruo* crops. In some areas they continue to divide responsibilities for different cultural operations for findi (*Digitaria exilis*), a low-yielding, early-maturing cereal which used to be a 'hunger season' crop but which had been abandoned in many parts of The Gambia by the 1970s.

The *kamanyango* (called *chukuno* in some areas, such as the Baddibous) is a field cultivated by a woman or junior man in the household, the disposal rights belonging to the cultivator. Household heads also cultivate crops on their own account but these fields are simply referred to as the 'household head's fields'. Mandinka men usually cultivate groundnuts on their *kamanyangos* and a few grow sorghum and millet; irrigated rice is becoming increasingly popular as a *kamanyango* crop. Women cultivate swamp or rainfed rice on the *kamanyango* as well as on the *maruo* and many outside observers have failed to appreciate the different destinations of these two crops.

(iii) Organisation of Labour

Men's *maruo* crops are normally cultivated by the *dabada*, a term which may be used in several ways. The primary meaning is a male agricultural labour group, and in the past probably consisted largely of male slaves and a few free-born men. It therefore excluded the old, the sick, young boys and all women. However, the word is also used to refer to all these categories, who are socially and sometimes financially dependent on the economically active men in the *dabada*. In this context, a man might say that he has a *dabada* even when he works alone. Women working together sometimes refer to their own work group as a *dabada*, although the word *sinkiro* (a kitchen, cooking unit) is much more common.

Men's *kamanyango* crops are sometimes cultivated by the *dabada*, in order of seniority of *dabada* members. This may be disadvantageous to the most junior men as their fields are often not reached until well after the optimum cultivation time, and a particularly zealous man would not get all the benefits of his extra hard labour. So it is becoming increasingly common for men to cultivate their kamanyangos alone, or with the help of various other forms of additional labour which are also available for the *maruo*. The most important of these are:

—'strange farmers': rainy season migrants from the Senegambia, Mali, Guinea Bissau and Guinea Conakry who help their hosts for about three days a week in return for food, lodging and the loan of land on which to cultivate a groundnut crop of their own.
—dry season migrant workers: they lift and thresh their hosts' groundnut crops for two to three days a week or do repair and construction work around the compound in return for food and lodging, after which they lift and thresh other farmers' crops for contract cash payments.
—contract and daily wage labour.
—reciprocal labour (not common for men).
—*kafo* labour: large work groups who are fed by the host and, in the case of the men's *kafos*, given a cow or cash.[2]

Women's labour is organised within the *sinkiro*. Like the word *dabada*, this is also a complex term with several meanings. The word refers to a group of women who rotate duties for cooking, usually for two days at a time, as well as the entire group of people, men and women of all ages, for whom they cook.

The *sinkiro* is usually headed by a man, although it is becoming increasingly acceptable for an elderly widow to head her own *sinkiro*. In Saruja in 1977–8 one woman was a *sinkiro* head. This means that although a *sinkiro* is normally dependent on a *dabada* or male work force, it is not necessarily so. The compound, the basic residential unit among the Mandinka, may consist of one or more *dabadas*. In Saruja the largest number of *dabadas* per compound was six and the average was 1.7. Each *dabada* in turn may have one or more *sinkiros*. In Saruja in most cases a *dabada* had only one *sinkiro*.

There are two principal reasons for this division of *dabadas* and *sinkiros* in a compound. First, the prevalent practice of polygamy combined with virilocal marriage, and the custom for married sons to remain in their father's compound, means that married brothers, particularly on the death of their father, often prefer to have their own *dabada* and/or *sinkiro*. Sometimes quarrels between wives necessitate separate *sinkiros* for the wives or groups of wives of a single man. Second, strangers, more distant relatives and Koranic students living in a compound usually want their own *sinkiros*, if not their own *dabadas*.

Women's *maruo* cultivation is organised within the *sinkiro* unit. In Saruja, the more common practice was for each married woman to cultivate her own *maruo* fields, helped by her unmarried daughters and young daughters-in-law. The latter gradually take over all their mother-in-law's responsibilities for the *maruo*. Most women also cultivate their own *kamanyangos*. In several *sinkiros* the women all worked together on the *maruo*; some cultivated their own *kamanyangos* while others farmed a common *kamanyango*, dividing the crop after the harvest. Women also have access to additional, non-*sinkiro* labour, especially reciprocal and *kafo* labour.

(iv) Control of the Crops and Crop Revenues

The men's *maruo* crops are controlled and stored by the *dabada* head. If the *dabada* has more than one *sinkiro* and he is not the head of them all, he divides the crop between the *sinkiros* after the harvest. Each *sinkiro* head allocates the grain to the women on some regular basis, often daily or every two days since this is the period of a woman's cooking duties. Each married woman who cultivates her own *maruo* crop stores the rice in her personal, often locked, storeroom, using it when it is her turn to cook. If all the *sinkiro* women work together on the *maruo* crops, the most senior woman usually stores the rice, measuring it out for the other women when it is their turn to cook.

The *kamanyango* crops, on the other hand, belong to the cultivator and both men and women control their own. A few women do not have separate *maruos* and *kamanyangos* but after the harvest take part of the crop for themselves, and use the rest for food.

The practice for men and women to cultivate their own crops and control the product appears to be long-standing. Moore commented [*Moore, 1738:vi*] that 'the Crops are the Properties of those who have tilled that Ground', a right which also belonged to women:

> ... and the Women busy in cutting their Rice; which, I must remark, is their own Property; for, after they have set by a sufficient Quantity for Family Use, they sell the Remainder, and take the Money themselves, the Husband not interfering. The same Custom they observe too in regard to the Fowls, which they breed up in great Quantities, when they find they can get Markets for them. [*Moore, 1738:139–40*]

Crops or the revenues from the *kamanyangos* are used partly to provide gifts and expenses for marriages, naming ceremonies, circumcision and funerals, for food for drumming and dancing parties, as well as for food for reciprocal and *kafo* agricultural labour groups. Both men and women buy most of their own clothes, and between them the clothes for their children; men try to buy their wives some cloth each year – if the harvest is good. Women pay for the tractor ploughing for their rice fields (though their husbands sometimes give them money for some of the fields, especially the *maruos*), the cooking condiments and meat or fish needed for the lunch for their reciprocal labour groups, any wage labour they employ, as well as small personal expenditures such as medicines, perfumes, serving bowls, jewellery for themselves and their daughters, cooking condiments and sometimes meat and vegetables for the *sinkiro*, the dowries for their daughters when they transfer to their husbands' compounds which consist of clothes, sheets, pots and pans. Young men nowadays may have to pay part, if not all, of their marriage payments, a function which traditionally is the responsibility of the *sinkiro* head. In theory the *dabada* head is supposed to pay for the seeds, fertilisers and tools for the *maruos* of all the men and women under him – a duty which he cannot or does not always agree to fulfil and the individual members have to provide for themselves.

In addition, men and women sometimes own cattle, sheep, goats and poultry, which they breed for sale, to be eaten on special occasions, or to be kept as an investment.

(v) Ownership and Control of Land

The key principle is that rights to use uncleared land are vested in the whole community and anyone who needs land may, with the permission of the village head, clear as much as he or she needs. Once cleared and cultivated, this land belongs to the person or persons who cleared it and the ownership rights may be given away or inherited by their heirs. The upland is either owned or controlled by men while women have ownership or secure use-rights to rice land. There are four different forms of ownership.

(i) Compound land, which cannot be alienated from the compound, and to which all compound members have use-rights. The compound head, his *dabada* and *sinkiro* have the right to some of the best land. This means that if a compound head dies, these fields are taken over by his successor (who is most commonly a brother) and the latter's *dabada*. This often leads to a redistribution of all the compound land according to the new hierarchy of *dabadas* and *sinkiros*.

If a compound splits up, the land is divided between compound members and descendants of members who had originally cleared it. Strangers who had settled after the compound had established rights to its land and had therefore not taken part in the clearing, would not be entitled to a share.

(ii) Land owned by individuals. A man or woman may establish personal ownership rights to land by the act of clearing and bringing it under cultivation. No relative or member·of his or her compound or lineage (*kabilo*) has any rights over that land which may be given away or inherited by the owner's children.

(iii) Land attached to certain offices. Land may be attached to the office of village, compound or lineage head. It is used by the office-holder or his wives and dependants but cannot be alienated from the office.

(iv) Lease land. This is land which has been acquired by the government from farmers for the purposes of development. An extensive area known as Jahali Swamp was obtained in 1950 and leased to the Gambia Rice Farm, a commercial enterprise set up by the Colonial Development Corporation. Following the failure of this scheme in the early 1950s, the land was leased to women rice farmers under a series of share cropping arrangements. None was successful as returns to

the farmers were no higher than on other land and since 1965 women from nine villages, including Saruja, have cultivated this land without paying any rent.

Rights to land owned by individuals may be transferred by gift or inheritance. Inheritance practices do not follow Islamic principles but continue the earlier custom whereby privately owned upland suitable for groundnuts and coos (sorghum and millet) is retained among men, passing from father to sons, and rice land is owned by women and inherited by their daughters. Older children tend to inherit more than their siblings. If there are no children, brothers and sisters act as residual heirs. Although a person owning land may give it away to whomever he or she wishes, in practice it is normally given to sons and daughters in advance of inheritance, or to sons-in-law, daughters-in-law or other close relatives. This inheritance pattern is further complicated by a marriage residence pattern of patrilocality, or the bride moving to the village of her husband. If the woman marries within her own village, as happens quite commonly, then there is no problem and the daughter inherits rice land from her mother according to custom. However, if the daughter marries outside the village, which can be a distance of more than 10 miles away, in theory her mother is not allowed to give her any land. Theoretically a woman's land should be reserved for village-resident daughters or daughters-in-law, but sometimes this precept is ignored.

The Mandinka land tenure system has an implicit notion of 'ownership for use'. Land which an individual owner no longer needs, whether for reasons of sickness, old age or because the area is too large to cultivate, is usually given away. If individuals or compounds have more land than they can use for one or more seasons, and if it is not under fallow, they lend it to other members of their compounds or to other villagers with whom they may have no ties of kinship or even friendship. Later settlers in a village often have no compound or private land of their own and their dependence on others for seasonal loans results in considerable insecurity. Land used to be lent for indefinite periods, which lessened this insecurity. However, attempts by farmers to claim the ownership rights to land which they had only been lent has led the owners to insist on seasonal loans.

The custom of 'ownership for use' demands that land should not be rented or sold. As a result of increasing land pressure, particularly around Banjul where commercial values are stronger, there have been a number of land sales in recent years. The prohibition on renting land is usually adhered to in the rural areas, with the exception of irrigated land which is openly rented since it is 'new'. Other land is sometimes rented in secret. In one case which came to the notice of the Saruja elders in 1977, the owner was 'advised' not to ask for money, advice which he accepted. However, many men told me that they gave 'kola' when they negotiated the loan of land. Since the expression may mean literally the traditional gift of kola nuts or the now accepted substitute of 'money for kola', the distinction between this gift and rent is blurred and is growing increasingly tenuous.

III. WOMEN'S ECONOMIC RIGHTS UNDERMINED

Historical sources suggest that the reciprocal rights and duties in the farming system were fairly allocated between men and women in the pre-colonial period. However, there are three reasons why men have moved into a more advantageous position during the nineteenth century, two of which stem directly from colonial policies.

First, groundnut production expanded rapidly after 1830 as the colonial powers sought to suppress the Atlantic slave trade, making it more profitable for chiefs and larger farmers to purchase the slaves and exploit their labour in groundnut production. Both small and larger farmers also responded to commercial incentives: attractive prices combined with a sudden influx of European goods available on credit to groundnut farmers. Towards the end of the century, the imposition of hut taxes forced farmers to grow a cash crop. Men took over the groundnut crops which had hitherto been grown in compound gardens while women continued to grow low-value rice which they sold or bartered in the village or surrounding region but for which there was no European demand. If men increased their groundnut production at the expense of their food crops, they fulfilled their contribution to the *sinkiro* by purchasing food and local or imported rice with their groundnut revenues. It should, however, be emphasised that men's control of the cash crop revenues brought them a parallel increase in their power within the family.

Second, the development policies of the colonial government from the end of the nineteenth century onwards were designed to promote cash crop production. After experimenting unsuccessfully with cotton, kola nuts, rubber, timber and fruit trees, the government concentrated on groundnuts, introducing higher yielding seeds, fertilisers, machinery and improved marketing structures. This substantially increased male farmers' incomes by improving yields and reducing labour which, given the fact that there was surplus land, led to an expansion in the total area under groundnuts. To some extent this increase was at the expense of men's food crops, for which there was declining demand in the twentieth century. The market for rice, the preferred staple, was growing in importance and the gap between demand and local production was being increasingly met by imports. Despite the rapidly mounting rice imports, very little was done to help women rice farmers, except for the construction of some causeways and the introduction of tractor ploughing in the 1950s on land not affected by early tidal flooding from the river. While tractor ploughing led to an expansion of the area under cultivation, continued reliance on low-yielding varieties grown with traditional techniques of transplanting, weeding and harvesting, increased labour bottlenecks for these operations and productivity remained low.

Third, the spread of Islam in the second half of the nineteenth century led to, and then reinforced, female subordination to male social and economic controls.

IV. CONFLICTING INTERESTS BETWEEN MEN AND WOMEN

By 1965, the year of The Gambia's independence, women had become economically disadvantaged relative to men. However, they do have important rights to their own land and crops, and therefore some economic independence which they may well need to defend. For this reason, planners need to be aware of the conflicting interests between men and women within the household and the ways in which men sometimes take advantage of women's social and economic dependence on them. There are three main areas in which Mandinka women are vulnerable to exploitation by men, areas in which development projects should aim to protect women's rights. These are discussed below and cover women's rights to land, their own crops, and adequate nutrition.

(i) Land Ownership Rights

Although both men and women have a right to clear land which they then own, in practice men often try to prevent women from exercising this right. This propensity emerged frequently in my interviews in Saruja and other villages in MacCarthy Island Division: men time and time again denied that women owned rice land, insisting either that men owned the land themselves or that it belonged to the compound and was therefore under male control. Women, on the other hand, claimed that they owned much of the land they cultivated and had secure rights to use compound land. In fact, compound rice land is generally administered by women, with older women taking the initiative in transferring their compound fields to young women marrying into the compound. Compound heads usually only assert their authority in disputes, cases of unfair distribution of the land by the women, or if women die before transferring their land. However, they do have ultimate responsibility for compound land and act vigorously to prevent it from being alienated from the compound.

This underlying tension between men and women with regard to the control of rice land has also been noted by other researchers. Rahman[3] gave a particularly graphic account of men's attempts to block women's access to land in Genieri, Lower River Division, in 1949. A meeting of village men was called to discuss land issues at a time when Genieri women were busy clearing and marking out boundaries to new rice fields. The men were determined to impose their authority on the women and take over responsibility for the clearing. The reason for this was spelt out by the village head:

> If women mark the land and divide it, it will become 'women's property', so that when the husband dies or when he divorces his wife, the wife will still retain the land, which is wrong. Women must not own land.

It is clear from the above quotation that women have a customary right to own land, a right which men will curtail in their own self-interest, and with no other justification than a purely emotive belief that it is 'wrong' for women to own land. Planners should be aware that if they only ask men about customary land tenure practices, they may get a biased and inaccurate account which excludes mention of women's rights. Moreover, if new or improved rice land is made available to a village, the men may well plan concerted action to monopolise the ownership rights, denying women a share.

(ii) Women's Rights to the Rice Crops

In principle, women can dispose of their *kamanyango* rice as they wish. However, in practice they may have to give it to the *sinkiro* if the *maruo* crops are poor or fail entirely.

Sometimes the men's coos crops are in short supply as men neglect these in favour of groundnuts. This is most liable to happen in *sinkiros* with a relatively large number of women [*Haswell, 1975:42*]. In such cases, men are expected to buy their wives' and other village women's *kamanyango* rice out of their groundnut revenues, to compensate for their own lower food crop production. However, if the harvest is unexpectedly poor or if they have personal needs which they regard as more pressing, they tend to insist that their wives use the *kamanyango* rice for the *sinkiro*, refusing to pay the women for it and forbidding them to sell it elsewhere. Since men are under no obligation to tell their wives how much they have received for their groundnuts, and women accept their husbands' authority as prescribed by Islam, the women can only acquiesce. Obviously if there were some exceptional reason why their husband could not pay for the rice, the women would not object. This is not always the case: there was one extreme example in Saruja when a man refused to buy his wives' *kamanyango* rice or let them sell it in the village. They were forced into debt for various necessary personal expenditures and to employ someone to harvest a field which they could not manage themselves because of illness. Their husband then went to Mecca that same season at very great expense.

Women's rights to their *kamanyango* and *maruo* crops are sometimes denied at divorce. By custom they should retain all the *kamanyango* rice and enough of the *maruo* rice to meet their own food needs until the next harvest. If the divorce is not amicable, a woman's claim may be overruled by her husband unless her own family lives in the village or nearby and can support her.

(iii) Nutrition

Studies have shown that rural pregnant and lactating women, and young children, have a calorie intake that is about 75–80 per cent of the WHO/FAO standard requirements, while rural men usually have a roughly adequate intake. This largely stems from the fact that men and women eat separately: the women serving the food feel obliged to give more of the nutritious sauces, meat and fish to the men while they satisfy their hunger on the bulky but lower-calorie staple. Since men control most of the cash revenues in the *sinkiro* and are already relatively well fed, they see no need to spend more on food for their wives and children. The fact that women in any case buy basic cooking ingredients such as onions, oil and tomato puree out of their own money, to supplement what their husbands provide, and will buy meat and fish if they have the money, underlines the importance of women's independent source of income.

V. THE IRRIGATED RICE DEVELOPMENT PROJECTS

An estimated 6,686 acres in MacCarthy Island Division and Upper River Division were developed for double-cropped irrigated rice between 1966–79. There were three similar schemes: the Taiwanese Agricultural Mission (1966–74), the World Bank Agricultural Development Project (1973–76) and the Agro-Technical Team of the People's Republic of China (1975–79).

In the initial project the Taiwanese Mission established an organisational procedure which was unquestioningly followed by subsequent missions. The Taiwanese technicians assumed that the local subsistence production system was based on a household which was a unified unit of production directed and controlled by a single male head. This was undoubtedly the way production was organised in Taiwan, but clearly did not fit local realities in Gambia, as has been shown above in Section II.

In each project, technical teams designed irrigation schemes in units of about 30 acres. Farmers were responsible for clearing and levelling the land, and helped with the construction of bunds and canals. Small diesel pumps were installed to raise water from the river. The Taiwanese provided the pumps, power tiller and pedal threshing machines free of charge, and farmers were given free seeds, fertilisers, ploughing, oil and diesel for the first crop. The World Bank project created co-operative Rice Growers' Societies through which farmers were given loans for the capital equipment and the seasonal inputs. A 10 per cent per annum interest charge was levied on both types of loan, the seasonal loan due for repayment at the end of each cropping season and the capital loan in annual instalments over a five year period. Since many farmers defaulted in these repayments and government running costs were high, the Chinese concentrated on developing new areas and the Department of Agriculture experimented with a different system of credits and direct charges. The capital equipment was provided free. Farmers had to pay cash for power tilling but they could get seasonal loans for seeds, fertilisers and a new water charge of Dalasi 100 (£25) per acre per crop to cover pump running and maintenance costs. Since the end of these development projects the Department of Agriculture is continuing its seasonal loans, to which an additional loan for power tilling was added in 1980.

VI. EFFECTS OF THE PROJECTS ON WOMEN

The technical teams implementing the three projects set out to contact the male household heads and invite their participation. The latter were offered the credits or free gifts of inputs which were an essential inducement in a country in which most farmers are chronically short of money and often heavily in debt as the rainy season progresses. These men, with the help of junior men in their *dabadas*, cleared the land, thereby establishing ownership rights to it, implicitly excluding women.

Saruja was short of land suitable for irrigation and cleared 38 acres, borrowing an additional 38.5 acres from two neighbouring villages. Saruja men cleared and developed this land also, claiming secure rights to use the borrowed land indefinitely, rights which are being inherited by their heirs or given away to other Saruja men if the cultivator moves from the village. Out of a total of 121 *sinkiros*, 66 *sinkiro* heads had no irrigated land while the other 55 owned or controlled almost all the 76.5 acres. Only 11 other men and four women had any irrigated land: seven of the men had less than half an acre and the women all had under a quarter of an acre. Two of the women had been given their plots by brothers, one by her father and one had inherited from her father because she had married a man in her father's compound. Almost all of the *sinkiro* heads had less than 1.5 acres and only four men had over 4 acres.

Although women had been effectively excluded from owning irrigated land and receiving the credits necessary for cultivating irrigated rice on their own account, their labour, particularly for transplanting and weeding, was nonetheless crucial for the success of the projects. Under the customary division of labour, women were under no obligation to work for their husbands. Since the latter were dependent on skilled female labour, a number of changes in remuneration and labour organisation have emerged to accommodate this new male demand for female labour.

(i) Women's Wage Labour

Women's customary duties and rights with respect to the *maruo* and *kamanyango* crops have in practice served to protect them from demands by their husbands to provide additional, free labour on men's irrigated rice fields. In order to secure female labour, men have been forced to pay village women cash wages. They are also obliged to pay their own wives' wages unless they substitute these for presents or the loan of an irrigated plot on which the women can grow a crop of their own.

However, women turn out to be a cheap source of labour: the village daily wage rate in Saruja and nearby villages for men varies between Dalasi 2.00–2.50,[4] while the women's is Dalasi 1.50–1.75. Women are paid Dalasi 2.00 for work on Kajakati Island since many hesitate to cross the river in small, unstable canoes, particularly if they have to take their young children or babies with them.

As few women are able to borrow irrigated rice land and even fewer own plots, there is considerable supply of female labour, particularly in the dry season when women do not have many other income-earning opportunities. In contrast, male labour is in short supply as men have greater opportunities to work at the nearby Sapu Agricultural Station where the official minimum wage rate is Dalasi 3.50 a day. Men are also less socially constrained to remain in the village and have a tradition of travelling to the capital, other parts of the Senegambia and, increasingly, abroad in search of work. The short supply of male labour, combined with abundant female labour serves to keep wages for women low relative to those for men.

(ii) Men's Control of Irrigated Rice Crops

A substantial proportion of the irrigated land is cultivated as *kamanyangos*, with men paying in cash or kind for female and additional male labour. The richer men sell most of this rice and reinvest in their private businesses such as trading and money lending. Others reserve the rice for *sinkiro* consumption, saving for their personal use the groundnut money they formerly spent on rice.

Some farmers regard the irrigated rice as a *maruo* crop, perhaps selling a small quantity, since the general prohibition on the sale of *maruo* crops is less strong with this 'new' crop. Women will usually be expected to work on the *maruo*. In many cases the men still give them wages and presents or lend them land since the women's labour in producing extra rice enables the men to save on the money they used to spend on rice. If men expect their wives to help for nothing, the women's work-load may become intolerably high on top of their demanding domestic duties while the men benefit from free labour and increased personal leisure.

(iii) Women's Work Choices in the Rainy Season

If women are unable to borrow irrigated plots to cultivate for themselves in the dry season, they have few other means of earning money and are eager to do wage labour for men. However, in the rainy season women have the alternative of growing their own rainfed and tidal swamp rice. Planners have tended to regard this rice purely as a subsistence crop and have underestimated the amount of local rice which is sold or bartered, and therefore the importance of this income to women.

The consequence of this is that if men need female labour for transplanting and weeding, they have to wait until Wednesdays or Fridays, days on which women traditionally do not go to their own fields. The short supply of female wage labour at this time of year does not, however, force up wage rates for the demand is equally low. Many men gave as one of the major reasons for not growing a rainy season crop the fact that they cannot afford to employ labour in the rains.

(iv) Women's Perceptions of the Irrigated Rice Projects

While the research did not specifically survey women's attitudes to the rice irrigation project, they sometimes voluntarily discussed among themselves or with me their feelings about the project. Two attitudes emerged. Firstly they all felt seriously disillusioned. When the Taiwanese technicians made their initial contacts with the village, the women were greatly excited because it was thought that the technicians were coming with the purpose of improving the women's rice production. As it gradually became apparent that the technicians intended only to deal with men and that women as primary producers of rice were to be passed over, the women were greatly disappointed.

The second attitude that emerged from these spontaneous discussions was the fact that women are very eager to have the opportunity to grow irrigated rice in the dry season on their own account and often expressed this in word and action. Women would badger male relatives to lend them irrigated plots for the season. It was very clear that they much prefer to grow their own rice than to work for wages on men's rice plots.

VII. CONCLUSIONS

The government saw the irrigated rice project as a means of achieving its major policy aim of self-sufficiency in food production by 1980. However, imports of clean rice have risen from an annual average of 8,700 tonnes between 1962–66 (the years immediately preceding the projects), to an average of over 20,000 tonnes a year between 1970/71–1978/9. By the end of the 1970s, production of irrigated rice was around 10,000 tonnes of paddy a year (the equivalent of about 6,500 tonnes of clean rice).

There is no doubt about the value of introducing a new dry season crop to farmers who had hitherto been entirely dependent on a single rainy season crop. However, more effective projects would have been devised had the planners first studied the existing farming system and particularly women's role within it, with a view to improving it instead of grafting onto it a cultivation system which was based on the joint family farm in Taiwan. Such an approach would have avoided some of the deficiencies of the projects and should also have convinced planners of the advantages to be gained in terms of increased national rice production by improving women's traditional rice.

The irrigated rice projects would have benefited in three ways from women's direct involvement. First, considerable areas in MacCarthy Island Division and Upper River Division were developed on land which floods in the rainy season. Since no drainage systems were constructed, much of this land is unsuitable for cultivation under controlled 'irrigated' conditions in the rainy season. Water control was only directed at irrigating these fields during the dry season and not to draining them in the rainy period. This has made them unsuitable for the cultivation of the short-stemmed but less hardy 'improved' varieties of rice during rainy season. These plots, which are unwanted by men, are left to women without swamp land to farm with indigenous varieties of rice which are more tolerant of deep and fluctuating water levels. If women had been involved in the design of these schemes, the technicians would have benefited from their considerable experience and could have developed more appropriate irrigation and drainage systems.

Second, while men are eager to grow a dry season crop, in the rainy season they find it easier to earn a similar return to their labour for groundnuts [Dey, 1980:349–51], a crop which is more conveniently inserted in their upland cereal cropping calendar. Women, on the other hand, are already growing rice: they could, without difficulty, cultivate some fields under irrigated conditions and others under rainfed or tidal conditions.

Third, the technique of line transplanting and weeding introduced by the projects require 5–10 people in a plot at a time. Few men have the resources to employ so many people in the rains. Women, however, can call on their reciprocal labour groups, whose financial cost is limited to the lunch provided by the crop owner.

Since little has so far been done to improve the productivity and overall national production of women's swamp rice, there are many areas in which a start could be made. The most obvious are the provision of high-yielding, disease-resistant seeds, fertilisers, pesticides, sickles, threshing machines, causeways and access roads, tractor and power tilling services, extension and bunds along portions of the river to control flooding. Such improvements could not be introduced piece-meal but would have to be part of a calculated plan as the following example shows.

At present women have to cut each individual panicle with a small knife and headload the bundles of rice out of the field across rickety bridges and narrow footpaths which are inaccessible to donkey carts. This method is nonetheless the most convenient for two reasons. First, in the absence of compact mechanical threshing machines, it is sometimes impossible to thresh rice in the field. The traditional method is to beat the rice with a stick. This requires space and is difficult in fields which are still flooded. Second, indigenous rice varieties are tolerant of the uncontrolled water levels in the swamps but are subject to severe lodging. It is far easier to harvest these with a small knife than with a sickle. On the other hand, this method of harvesting is laborious and creates serious labour bottlenecks. This in turn means that the rice is often over-ripe before it is harvested, which leads to shattering and a considerable loss of grain. Improvements in harvesting and threshing techniques would therefore have to be part of a comprehensive planned programme introducing water control, suitable seed varieties and access roads.

By failing to take into account the complexities of the existing farming system and concentrating on men to the exclusion of women, the irrigated rice projects have lost in the technical sense that valuable available female expertise was wasted. Furthermore, investment was focused on relatively expensive capital-intensive irrigation schemes when striking results might have been obtained by a few simple improvements in women's rainfed and swamp rice. Finally, by excluding women, the projects have increased women's economic dependence on men who now control an additional food and cash crop, and thereby heighten their vulnerability in an increasingly unstable and changing rural economy.

NOTES

1. Women of other ethnic groups, for example, the Wolofs, also grow groundnuts.
2. See [Dey, 1980:185–96] for an account of these forms of labour organization.
3. [Rahman, 1949]. These notes on land tenure, written for D. P. Gamble by A. K. Rahman, were very kindly made available to me by Dr. Gamble.
4. Dalasi 4 = £1.

REFERENCES

Dey, J. M., 1980, 'Women and Rice in The Gambia: The impact of irrigated rice development projects on the farming system', Ph.D. thesis, University of Reading.
Haswell, M. R., 1975, The nature of poverty. London: Macmillan.
Moore, Francis, 1738, Travels into the inland parts of Africa. London: E. Cave.
Rahman, A. K., 1949, Unpublished notes on Land Tenure in Genieri.

Developing Women's Cooperatives: An Experiment in Rural Nigeria

by Patricia Ladipo *

This study focuses on the experiences of two groups of Yoruba women who tried to organise themselves along modern cooperative lines. The progress of the first group which tried to adhere to government regulations, is compared to that of the second, which moulded its own rules. Cohesion, personal development, and financial growth were found to be greater in the self-regulating group. Implications for cooperative policy are discussed.

INTRODUCTION

This study reports the experiences of two groups of Yoruba women who tried to organise themselves along the lines of multi-purpose cooperatives. This type of institution was originally developed in Nigeria to protect cocoa producers, mostly men, from the exploitation of foreign middlemen [*Ijere, 1977:6*]. Although multi-purpose cooperatives eventually evolved to serve other functions in addition to cocoa marketing, they were still viewed by cooperative officials as farmers' or men's institutions in 1976 when this study began. Thus, the idea of developing women's multi-purpose cooperatives was quite a new one.

The study took place in the context of a rural development project which was, itself, experimental. The Isoya Rural Development Project was started in 1969 by the University of Ife as a pilot project in integrated rural development. That is, in addition to the objective of improving the living conditions of rural people in the area around the University, the project was meant to serve as a laboratory for testing and teaching approaches to rural development. Because experimentation was built into the project, programming was flexible and, as will be shown, it was possible to learn from, and at times compensate for, errors.

The project included programmes in agriculture, intermediate technology, home economics, and adult literacy. However, from the start there was a heavy emphasis on agricultural programmes and by 1972, a high yielding variety of yellow maize was successfully introduced as a cash crop. Previously, cocoa and kola nuts were the major cash crops, with food crops including a local variety of white maize, playing minor roles in the cash economy of the area. As is common in Yoruba land, women in the project villages had marketed food crops, including maize, while the greatest volume of the cash crops were marketed by men [see *Berry 1975:132* and *Boserup, 1970:19*]. The new maize was not initially

* The author wishes to acknowledge the insights and encouragement provided by Mr. D. O. Oyeyemi throughout this study and the kind cooperation of several officials of the Oyo State Ministry of Trade and Cooperatives.

accepted as food; it was in high demand as animal feed; and it was produced in commercial quantities. Thus it was perceived as a cash crop and its marketing was carried out by men's cooperatives which were organised, with the help of project staff, specifically to handle it.

Not only were women effectively excluded from marketing yellow maize, but in addition, the supply of local white maize almost vanished as increasing areas were put under cultivation of the new crop. In the years before contact with the development project, most of the women had evolved carefully balanced systems of marketing wherein they invested their own capital and energy in a sequence of crops, consumables and services over the seasonal growing cycle. Within the first two years of its inception, the maize project created a gap in the women s marketing cycles.[1] Much of the capital which should have been invested in maize was spent or directed to less profitable, untimely trades.

Many women found themselves in embarrassing situations which they began discussing with project staff in 1976. The women saw trade as almost the only route to economic self-sufficiency even though trade was usually based on an initial capital outlay given them by their husbands.[2] Many women who had already established their independence found themselves turning again to their husbands for capital. This was considered degrading and not very profitable since there were many other demands on the husbands' maize incomes. The level of frustration was heightened by the fact that the women saw clearly that the same crop which had upset their trading systems had also brought an unprecedented level of prosperity to the area. They saw that the local market for consumables and services was growing rapidly, but the capital for new investments had already been lost.

In pointing out their dilemma to project staff, women emphasized that they appreciated the goodwill and efforts of the staff. It appeared that they saw the maize programme as evidence of concrete achievement, while the home economics programme which had focused on nutrition was interpreted as evidence of a humane concern for their welfare. They saw their basic problem as one of money, and noted that the project had brought progress, literally 'marching forward' to the men while they as wives had been 'pulled backwards'. Several said that as a bird uses two wings to fly, so must a family use the progress of its husband and wife to get ahead. In short, women asked for a programme which would have economic benefits for them.

When project staff asked whether they could organise themselves into groups and work towards government recognition as the men were doing, there was an enthusiastic response: within a month, without staff involvement, the women of six villages met, established a headquarters at Isoya village, and elected a set of officers. They then sent for staff to guide them in their activities.

The major benefit of organising envisaged by the women was the possibility of qualifying for government aid in the form of credit and other facilities. In order to know how best to guide the group towards government recognition, staff investigated the government policies and guidelines relating to cooperatives. The current National Development Plan indicated that there were many types of cooperatives recognised, but that special attention would be given to the development of groups that could serve as organs of agricultural development. Such groups, designated as multi-purpose cooperatives, were meant to facilitate extension efforts, the introduction of new technology, and the dispersal and management of credit. [*Federal Republic of Nigeria, 1975:1:319–20, 71*]. Multi-purpose cooperatives were not new to the area: they had long been the institutions through which cocoa was marketed; and the farmers were developing their maize groups along multi-purpose lines. What was new was that such groups were to be favoured in terms of government assistance.

A list of the current requirements for government registration was provided by the State Ministry of Trade and Cooperatives. In addition to having officers and being governed by acceptable bye-laws, multi-purpose cooperatives were required to: have a minimum membership of fifty; deposit a minimum share payment of ten naira per person in the bank; organise a regular monthly savings scheme; undertake a group project; hold regular meetings; and keep records including various account books. Multi-purpose groups were also encouraged to develop their experience with credit by running an internal loan programme. The officer who supplied this information pointed out that most of the multi-purpose societies which were registered were large marketing associations. He doubted whether women could operate this type of organisation, and recommended that the women form a thrift and credit cooperative which differed from the multi-purpose type in that the book-keeping requirements were stricter, but no group project was required.

The policies and regulations of the government were reported to the women and the alternative types of cooperative were discussed. The group saw an opportunity for improving crop processing and storage through collective work and chose to organise along multi-purpose lines. Although they were awed by the list of requirements, many said that they could do what the men were doing, since, after all, the same staff who were helping the men would be helping them. Thus, in October 1976, the group which called itself *Irewolu*, headquartered at Isoya village, began to conduct its affairs according to government regulations.

Following the example of *Irewolu*, women in Aganran village organised themselves into a group called *Ifelodun* in February 1977. Since, by then, the first group had undergone considerable stress in trying to meet the requirements, staff decided that the second group should be allowed to adapt the regulations to suit its own situation. It was hoped that by starting with a more appropriate set of rules, the second society would build up a performance record that would qualify it for registration. Thus, an experiment was begun wherein there were two groups trying to reach the same goal of government recognition by different means.

Dennis [*1976*] made the criticism that most discussions on women and development assume development as a given process and focus on how best women can be adjusted to that process. She called for planning which would focus on adjustments to the process itself. The background to this study has shown that the women were forced to adjust to a given process, the maize programme. That situation is seen as regrettable, and could probably be avoided in the future. However, it did provide the opportunity for experimenting with another process, cooperative development. In this study, the first group, *Irewolu*, set about adjusting itself to the given requirements. The second group was encouraged to test ways by which cooperative procedures could be modified to suit the women's needs.

The purpose of this paper is to highlight the problems and potentials of the women in both groups, to compare the progress of the two groups, and to discuss the implications of this experiment for government cooperative policy. The study covers the first eighteen months of each group's activities. It draws on the groups' records and the field notes of the author who was one of the project staff working with and observing the groups.

INITIAL DIFFERENCES

Before looking at the performance of the women, it is important to note the differences inherent in the two groups as well as the differences in the regulations they used. The most obvious difference was in size of membership. *Ifelodun*, the second cooperative, had only 29 members which was almost all the women in one village. The original group, *Irewolu*, initially had 100 members which included the majority of women from six villages. These six villages were scattered over an area of about eight square miles and were connected by laterite roads which were seldom used by vehicles and which, in fact, were difficult to walk on for almost half the year.

A survey of the women's socio-economic characteristics showed that the groups were slightly different. Most of the women had had previous experience with formal organisations including religious groups, trade associations, savings societies, and associations of household (lineage) wives. However, participation had been higher among the *Ifelodun* members (where all but two had belonged to other societies) than in the *Irewolu* group where only 62 per cent had had experience with organisations and meetings. The proportion of members who had held official positions in other groups was 10 per cent in *Irewolu* and slightly higher in *Ifelodun* (15 per cent).

Although very few women in either group could read or write, the literacy rate was slightly higher in *Ifelodun* (19 per cent) than in *Irewolu* (13 per cent). *Irewolu* women tended to be younger than *Ifelodun* members. Half of the women in the larger group (*Irewolu*) were under thirty years of age and these included many teen-aged brides. In the smaller group (*Ifelodun*) there were no teen-agers and 79 per cent were over thirty.

Since women in this area have been found to build their enterprises over time by investing in increasingly capital intensive projects, the age differences suggested that there might be occupational differences between the two groups. It was found that petty or small-scale trade was the most common occupation among the members of the younger group and that only a quarter of them traded in kola nuts and cocoa. The reverse was found in *Ifelodun*, where only five members were petty traders and 45 per cent were produce buyers. The maize gap mentioned earlier was evident in both groups as maize was the least frequently mentioned commodity and was handled by older women who had no child-care duties and were free to trade outside the project area.

On examining the commodities sold in the two areas, one might conclude that *Ifelodun* women were more prosperous and had adjusted better to the absence of maize in their trading cycles. One explanation for this would seem to be that they were older and better established than the *Irewolu* women when the maize programme took effect. However, the survey also showed that more *Ifelodun* members engaged in services for pay. In fact, half of them worked as agricultural labourers, whereas none of the other group did. Another 20 per cent of the smaller group provided ready-to-eat meals for sale, compared to only 3 per cent of the larger group. Thus it may be that the women in *Ifelodun* had adjusted to the maize programme by participating in any ways they could, and then applying the proceeds to trade in other commodities.

In addition to trade and services, a third occupation was farming. Some women had inherited farms from their families of origin and since most of the women were not born into the project area, most of their land was outside of the locality. Because of this, most of these women were absentee landlords although a few contributed labour and management to the operations of their farms. In either case, the farms served as sources of income and more *Ifelodun* members had farms than did *Irewolu* members (40 per cent to 13 per cent respectively).

It was not possible to gather income data during the survey, primarily because cash flows fluctuated by season and by the periodic market calendar within seasons. The occupational data presented here may indicate that the smaller group was more prosperous or at least more enterprising than *Irewolu*.

However, judging from one of the societies' first activities, the choosing of names and officers, one would have assumed the larger group to be more dynamic. *Irewolu* means 'Good Things Come to the Town', and its members chose a president whom they felt could help bring them the good things of life. She was literate and well travelled and had a keen sense of the events which were modernising the country. As a non-native of the area and the only widow, she was in many ways less tied to the locality than the other members were. However, this fact plus her reputation as a Christian evangelist probably made her even more acceptable as a leader for the new organization.

In contrast, the president of *Ifelodun* seemed initially much more passive. She had never learned to read or write, rarely left the village, and never voiced an awareness of any event outside of her own community. She practiced her religion, Islam, within her home. She was rarely seen to exercise any influence on the conduct of meetings, but it was apparent that she had considerable authority, probably stemming from her role as the village's traditional midwife. It seems she was elected to ensure harmony and stability to a group whose name can be translated as, 'Friendship is Sweet'.

The inherent differences between the two groups form part of the background against which their later experiences can be evaluated. However, these differences were not seen as an adequate basis for assuming any differences in the economic or organizational potentials of the groups at the time the regulations were set up. Initially, the regulations of the two cooperatives differed in three aspects. The first of these was that *Ifelodun* was allowed to operate with its small membership of 29; it was not required to find additional members from other villages. Secondly, *Ifelodun* decided that the size of its minimum share payment should be five naira, or half the government requirement. Thirdly, *Ifelodun* members were allowed to withdraw their accumulated savings from the society during the 'hungry season' from April till June. As will be seen below, there were other adaptations made in the regulations followed by *Ifelodun* as the group's activities progressed. However, *Irewolu* members tried to adhere to the government regulations throughout.

COMMON EXPERIENCES

For both groups, the process of cooperative formation demanded changes in skills, concepts, habits, and attitudes. The extent of these changes indicated the distance between the women and the institution which was to help them progress.

A major obstacle was a general lack of experience with the bureaucratic world. A few of the women had had dealings with agricultural or cooperative officers, but the contact was infrequent and mediated through their husbands or other men. None of the women had ever dealt with a bank and their first experience illustrates the type of problem they faced. Project staff took the secretaries and treasurers to the bank to open accounts. All the way to town, the officers bolstered their courage by discussing what they had been told about the physical layout of the bank and by reminding themselves that, after all, their men had learned to deal with banks and they could, too. Inside the bank the women were terrified, but they finally walked out victoriously with their pass books. Thereafter, they banked with assurance and their prestige and self-esteem rose as a result.

Contact with machinery was another new and frightening experience. Men were used to handling a variety of machines including bicycles, motor bikes, and food mills; but the only women who were familiar with machinery were two who had used sewing machines. When the *Irewolu* members decided to purchase and operate a mechanical maize sheller as their group project, they faced several problems. First, they had to overcome their fear of the machine. Then they had to teach their muscles new patterns and rhythms of movement. Finally, they had to develop the skill to manage the sheller. All through this growing process they had to deal with the resentment of their husbands who felt the machine should properly belong to them.

The *Ifelodun* project which was a group maize and cassava farm did not entail the use of machinery. It showed that, as farm labourers and managers, the women had a good deal of experience with new farm methods and materials. However, like their *Irewolu* sisters, *Ifelodun* members faced opposition from the men who gave the group land from which the top soil had been scraped for road construction. The women were aware of the deficiency, but rationalised the choice of the site by saying that the purpose of the farm was to impress the government with their group work. It would be easier for officials to see a farm that was next to the main road.

As the groups marched into the domain of men, the secretaries were on the front-line, representing their societies to the concerned institutions. As a result they underwent more stress than the other members at the local level. They were under considerable pressure to attend all the meetings. While the other members could occasionally choose to attend a market on the meeting day and pay a fine for absence, the absence of the secretary meant that the meeting would not be held. At the meetings, the secretaries struggled to apply their inadequate and rusty writing skills to the job of taking minutes and writing receipts.

The most time-consuming part of the job occurred on non-meeting days when the secretaries tried to keep account books including personal ledgers, monthly analysis books, cash books, and general ledgers. The accounting which was mastered with difficulty by project staff was never entirely grasped by the secretaries who had only one year of post-primary education.

Furthermore, the elaborate accounts were seen as an unnecessary requirement by most of the members who, being illiterate, had developed a remarkable ability to commit financial records to memory. They did see the value of receipts, but that value was limited by the need to rely on others to read them. In order to allow everyone to participate in record keeping, savings receipts were given in the form of stamps.[3] This provided proof of payment and considerable incentive to save. It also enabled other members to take over one aspect of the secretaries' work.

The women appreciated that their secretaries were making sacrifices in terms of time, effort, and trading opportunities. Both groups voted to pay a fee (of about ten naira annually) to their secretaries, realising that compared to the fee they would have had to pay a secretary from the cooperative union, this was only a token.

The problem of providing secretarial skills highlights what was an easily discernible disadvantage the groups faced. There were other, less obvious ways in which the women were ill-equipped for participation in modern institutions. Most of the members had to develop new concepts, for example, new concepts of time. Although all the women knew about time of day, for most, the need to regulate their activities to the clock had been limited to the task of getting their children to school in the morning. The idea that to arrive at 10 a.m. for a 9 a.m. meeting was to arrive late was a totally foreign one and had to be learned. Calendar time was an even stranger concept. Women who were used to marking the year by rain, crops, and festivals found it difficult to plan towards loan repayment on a certain calendar date. Initially, dates had to be associated with known events, but later, that was not necessary.

Another conceptual problem was the apparent inability to remember long-term goals and the steps required to meet these goals. Time and again it seemed that the idea of government registration had been forgotten and replaced by more immediate goals to which the registration requirements actually served as impediments. For example, there was usually unanimous agreement to proposals that unqualified members be given loans or that absentee members should not be fined. Such proposals were always dropped when staff re-iterated the benefits of and requirements for registration. However, the reminder never came from within the group.

The president of *Irewolu* did remember the long-term goal and the relationship between it and the rules, but she also understood that members often had pressing problems which prevented them from behaving according to regulations. According to her own analysis, the problem was more basic than a lack of ability to remember rules. It was that individuals expected that their society should participate in or at least accommodate events in their own lives. She put it that the members might get sick, or lose their capital, or be faced with funeral expenses, but this governmental society, unlike all other societies didn't see such things. The society's ears were closed to personal difficulties, but the members ears were open.

From the time this discussion took place, staff made a conscious effort to activate a dual approach to cooperative participation. On the one hand, the records were to show adherence to regulations. On the other, members were to be encouraged to be charitable, to assist each other in meeting the requirements. This approach was used, for example, when one member had spent all her money on medical care for her son and was forced to default on her loan. The other members wanted to forgive the loan, but the requirements stated that the debtor's two sureties should pay it. It was felt that the whole society should absorb the disaster. This was done by individuals' contributing money to the sureties who then cleared the debt in the normal manner.

In another case, a member took a loan which she promptly shared with her two sureties. This was, evidently, a common practice. However, when the loan came due, she repaid only two-thirds of it, saying that one of the sureties had lost her own part of it. Fortunately, the other members were, by then, able to explain that the society was concerned with only one debtor and that the sharing of the loan was a personal matter.

This dual approach was effective in getting things done. It also helped women to develop the skill of differentiating between personal and official transactions. However, at the same time, it may have undermined the concept that the societies belonged to the women themselves, rather than to the government. In effect, the members learned how to bridge the gap between old and new ways of interacting, but the gap became more apparent in the process.

This is reflected in the changing attitudes of the women towards government and towards their groups. Although no survey was conducted on attitudes, much was learned from discussion and from the prayers used to open meetings.[4] Government, which was a frequent topic of prayer in the first few months of both groups' meetings, featured as a benevolent or stern father figure: 'God, please let us please the government'; 'Let the government be happy and open its hand to us'; 'God, don't let us annoy the government'; 'Don't let the government write us a letter'.

Later, government, as an unpredictable force, was gradually replaced in the prayers by a few known cooperative officials. The officials were seen on a level with the women themselves, and the requests were quite specific: 'God of heaven, the creator of all creatures, please take special care of your creature, Mr. X. Don't let his motor bike crash. Let him teach his wisdom to the secretary.' This change was more evident in the *Ifelodun* group which was progressing faster and therefore received more government attention. ·

As the cooperative officials became familiar and established their reputations as 'real people' and 'gentlemen', there was the hope that reciprocity would develop between them and the societies, and that the government regulations could be 'bent'. One prayer showed that the officials were seen as quite separate from the government: 'Let the government listen to Mr. X and open its eyes to us'. When they understood that the regulations were fixed, the groups paid more attention to the conduct of their business.

In the process, the outlooks of the groups towards themselves seemed to change and turn inwards. At first there were many comments and rousing prayers about finding the path to progress. Later, after the procedures had been more or less understood and accepted, the concern was with more mundane problems such as distributing the next set of loans. To some extent, this may have represented progress coincident with the women's increasing ability to deal with detail. However, it may also indicate a fading of idealism.

In this regard, it is worth considering the extent to which the men's attitudes towards the women's groups may have affected the women's own outlooks. After women in the two areas had decided that they wanted to form cooperatives, project staff discussed the idea with the farmers' groups. The farmers, who were used to participating in change, had been happy that something progressive might also reach their wives. In addition to this collective consent, each husband gave his individual consent for his wife to join the group.

In retrospect, it seems likely that the men based their approval on their previous experience with women's groups. Some known types of women's associations such as age sets were of a non-economic nature and posed no threats to male interests. Others, such as associations of household wives or women's religious groups were sub-units of male-dominated systems. Women's trade associations, which had some economic functions and some independence were far away in the town. In fact, the only local and economically oriented associations in which women had been seen participating had been savings and produce marketing associations, in which men outnumbered the women.

The cooperatives did not resemble any of these associations and men could easily have felt that the women's groups transgressed their boundaries. Perhaps more embarrassing than the women's incursions into mechanization and production was the fact that the women began to keep proper records long before the men's groups did. Indeed, the women's example spurred the men to start keeping accounts.

While there is very little direct evidence that the men were resentful, the minutes of meetings show that only in the later months were decisions postponed until husbands could be consulted. At the beginning, the men's advice had little substantive impact on the women's decisions, so perhaps the important aspect was just the asking for advice. As several women pointed out, 'This society stands by the permission of the men.' Both the staff and the members learned that the men's approval was conditional and a continuing process. Most of the time, by simply adopting a low profile, it was possible for the groups to proceed with what they wanted to do.

DIFFERENCES IN PROGRESS

There was one important issue in which the men's wishes prevailed against the wishes and capabilities of the majority of women. As mentioned earlier, *Irewolu* comprised members from six villages. The president was associated with Isoya village, but very few other Isoya women joined the society and the few who had joined rarely attended meetings. Early in the group experience, the other members wanted to remove the headquarters from Isoya and rotate it among their own villages. Later, they wanted to break the society into three branches with Isoya standing on its own. It was the men who stopped an amicable separation by insisting that Isoya maintain its traditional place as the most prominent village of the area.

Thus, *Irewolu* members were somewhat reluctantly joined together. There was the physical problem of getting to meetings. This affected attendance and undermined the confidence of each member that loans would be repaid and that she would find enough sureties to guarantee her own loan in the future. But perhaps a more basic problem was the physical and social distance that separated the villages. The women of the various villages had never interacted in other contexts. Because of this, they knew that their ability to apply sanctions was limited to the official procedures set out in their association's bye-laws. Such procedures were seen as foreign and a possible source of public disgrace for the whole society.

Ifelodun was a much more cohesive group. All the members were physically close. If meeting attendance was low, a group of members simply went round the village rousing women from their houses. Moreover, *Ifelodun* constituted a social group to which the women had belonged from the time they first married and moved to Aganran village. While all members were not equally esteemed and trusted, the society trusted its collective ability to predict the behaviour of all its members. There was also confidence that any undesirable behaviour could be controlled without resorting to official or governmental procedures.

The successful application of local social control was seen in one incident when public opinion and a local seer jointly determined that one member had stolen another's loan repayment. The alleged culprit was allowed to return the money without any loss of face and harmony was maintained in the society. *Irewolu* women did not have recourse to similar methods and perhaps this knowledge, more than any actual event, bred distrust.

In addition to fostering collective confidence, group cohesion seems to have built up personal confidence in *Ifelodun* members. This was illustrated by the members' innovative attempts to lighten the burden of their secretary. They said that while their secretary was the most educated among them, she was not the only literate member. They suggested that any member who could read and write numbers and sign her name should come forward to assist in the writing of receipts. Two women found the courage to volunteer. Thus, although it was contrary to normal procedures, part of the secretary's work was rotated between two women and three signatures appear on the records.

As a follow-up to this, the group asked that the project organise literacy and numeracy lessons in the village. This was done and fifteen members, including some who had never gone to school, took part. Optimism and cooperation pervaded the classes. People who refused to join were ridiculed but participants who were slow to learn were encouraged. Women rewarded each other's good performance with remarks such as, 'You will be our next secretary.' Indeed, the prospect of helping the group seemed to be the main factor motivating class efforts.

Although the possibility of rotating secretarial duties was presented to *Irewolu* women, there were no volunteers. Individuals who were known to be literate refused to help on the basis of youth, or of coming from too small a village. Their responses seemed to indicate both a lack of self-confidence and a lack of group commitment. It was not possible to interest *Irewolu* members in adult education classes.

So far, this has been a rather subjective account of the women's experiences in cooperative formation. Let us now look at the objective measures of group progress which are drawn from the minutes and financial records and which, therefore, are the facts available to government officials for evaluating the groups.

The size of the two groups has already been mentioned, but it is important to look at how many women were effective participants.

Although *Irewolu* originally had 100 women attending meetings, only 43 of them completed paying their ten naira shares. Another 8 members had partially completed share payments, so that the total number of committed members should be considered as 51. Had all these members bought shares, *Irewolu* would have just met the government requirement in terms of size. *Ifelodun's* membership was only 29, but all of the women owned five naira shares and may be considered active participants. In both societies, attendance at meetings was affected by seasonal activities and by attendance at festivals, ceremonies, and markets. Even so, *Ifelodun's* average attendance rate was 41 per cent compared with 29 per cent for *Irewolu*.

There were corresponding differences between the groups in terms of financial growth. *Irewolu* members who struggled to make their ten naira share payments did not progress well with their monthly savings programme: savings represented only 7 per cent of their total capital compared with 38 per cent for the group which was allowed to make smaller share payments. It was not possible for either group to enforce regular monthly savings in the sense that each woman should contribute the same amount, 50 kobo, every month. Staff tried to encourage *Irewolu* to meet the requirements for regular savings, but seasonal and personal fluctuations in income affected even the most committed members. In *Ifelodun*, on the other hand, women were allowed to vary their savings with a view to paying an average amount of 50 kobo monthly.

The issue of loan distribution provides a focal point for viewing many of the differences between the two groups. The problem of inter-village distrust in *Irewolu* has already been mentioned. It is interesting that the women themselves decided to solve this problem by distributing loans to villages based on the proportion of shares each village owned. Most of the women understood the principle of proportionality and were able to remember the distribution of shares and also to do the mental arithmetic needed to calculate the loan distribution. However, this approach did not really facilitate loan distribution because up-to-date savings were a requirement which few loan applicants met and because attendance was often so low that loan applicants could not always find sureties, particularly sureties from their own villages.

In the period covered by this study, less than half of the *Irewolu* women who were qualified to borrow money actually received loans: only 17 loans were made and loan interest contributed less than eight per cent to the total capital accumulated. *Ifelodun* members were able to begin their loan scheme much earlier than *Irewolu*, because it was easier for them to meet their share and savings requirements. Also, they trusted each other more and had a higher attendance rate which made it easier to provide sureties. Furthermore, the older and presumably better established women often ceded their turns for loans to younger, poorer members. *Ifelodun* distributed 52 loans which reached all of the members qualified to borrow. The contribution of loan interest to their total capital was about 12 per cent.

As a result of its savings and loan programme, *Ifelodun* members were able to compensate for a relatively small amount of share capital; their average contribution per head, per month was 82k. At *Irewolu*, a larger amount of share capital was available but underutilized and the mean rate of capital accumulated was only 65k per member per month.

The total capital of *Irewolu* and *Ifelodun* was ₦596 and ₦427 respectively. The women, who saw money as a resource to be worked, rightly understood that they could not afford to put the required ₦500 on deposit in the bank.

IMPLICATIONS

One of the limitations of this study was that only two societies were observed. Inherent differences between the two groups could not have predicted the different experiences, but may have affected the groups' progress. Obviously then, the results of this experiment should not be generalised, but they do raise practical issues for consideration by cooperative policy makers.

The first is the issue of group size. This experiment suggests that perhaps there should be no requirement concerning size, and that women should be allowed to form cooperatives within the bounds of existing social groups.

Book-keeping was found to be the most difficult and time consuming aspect of work for the members and secretaries of both societies and for the project staff. The teaching of accounting skills and the checking of accounts also took more of the cooperative officials' time than any other task. These findings, as well as the fact that the stamp scheme was easily understood and accepted by members, suggest that the use of stamps should be expanded to account for most of the transactions in cooperatives where the literacy rate is low.

Seasonal activities were important factors affecting both availability of cash and attendance at meetings. While it is understandable that the government should require evidence of consistent efforts, it may be that the concept of 'regular' should be modified so that it would indicate an established pattern of meetings or savings within the scope of a year, rather than indicating a monthly recurrence of activities.

Throughout the study, it was apparent that most of the women had very little cash available to them. The general lack of funds was evident in the fact that many women dropped out of *Irewolu* because they could not find the share money. It would also explain why some of the women were willing to share their loans three ways. The high value of money and the relatively greater success of the group which was allowed to make smaller share contributions suggest that perhaps the size of share payment should be decided by each group and that the government should encourage women to keep their money in productive use, rather than requiring them to deposit it in banks.

Finally, there are some practical implications to be seen in the groups' experiences with collective projects. *Irewolu's* experience indicates that there may be a limit to the number of changes that can be successfully introduced at one time. The experience of both groups indicates that more consideration could have been given to the attitudes of men. Limiting one's view to the immediate experiment, it would seem that both groups might have had fewer obstacles had they restricted their activities to marketing or 'women's work'. However, one cannot entirely ignore the background to this experiment. Women's roles could have been defined with the farmers, right from the inception of the maize programme, and planning could have ensured that women market the new crop.

In considering the implications just raised, it is important 'to note the second limitation of this study. That is, that the inputs of project staff and cooperative officials were of a very high order and not, as yet, likely to be replicated. Project staff spent about three man-days per month with each society and they co-opted a quite unusual level of assistance from government officials. Even so, after 18 months, neither society was ready for registration. This suggests that the manpower costs of preparing the women's groups for registration would be prohibitive if the process were to be attempted on a wide scale.

In this light, the present government registration requirements may be seen as limiting the number of eligible societies and thus limiting the work load of the Ministry of Trade and Cooperatives to managable limits. Any change in registration requirements that might open the cooperative movement to the majority of rural women would probably require a massive commitment of manpower and funds.

However, this study suggests that such a commitment is justifiable. The process of cooperative formation, though stressful, was found to be a developmental one which built skills and attitudes women need if they are not to be left behind in a modernising society. Furthermore, personal and group development were found to be facilitated in the situation where the regulations were adapted to the women's needs. It may be that the women were more willing to adapt themselves to a process over which they had some control.

NOTES

1 The differential impact of rural development programmes on men and women has been widely documented. See the reviews by Pala and FAO. However, most of the examples deal with effects on farming rather than marketing activities of women.
2. For a comprehensive discussion of Yoruba women's trading activities vis-à-vis family and social relations, see Sudarkasa, [1973]. Although her study was conducted in a town, her findings on the importance of trade have been confirmed in the project villages.
3. The OXFAM Save-Way stamps and cards were used for this purpose.
4. It should be mentioned that at each meeting, the women nominated someone to pray. The opening prayers served several functions: they provided an acceptable way of stating deeply felt ideas or fears; they focused the minds of the participants on the issues to be discussed; they provided a neutral way of warning members that unacceptable behaviour had been noticed; they awarded praise for dedicated service; and they helped build a cohesive and courageous spirit among the women.

REFERENCES

Berry, S. S., 1975, *Cocoa, Custom and Socio-Economic Change in Rural Western Nigeria*, Oxford: Clarendon Press.
Boserup, E., 1970 *Woman's Role in Economic Development*, London: George Allen and Unwin.
Dennis, C., 1976, 'Women and Development: What Kind of Development?,' *National Conference on Nigerian Women and Development in Relation to Changing Family Structure*, Nigeria: University of Ibadan.
Federal Republic of Nigeria, 1975, *Third National Development Plan*, Lagos: Federal Ministry of Economic Development.
FAO, 1975, 'The Role of Women in Rural Development', Rome.

Ijere, M. O., 1977, *Modernising Nigerian Cooperatives*, Lagos: Fred Atoki Publ. Co.
Pala, A. O., 1976, *African Women in Rural Development: Research Trends and Priorities*, OLC Paper No. 12, Overseas Liaison Committee.
Sudarkasa, N., 1973 *Where Women Work: A Study of Yoruba Women in the Marketplace and in the Home*, Ann Arbor: University of Michigan Press.